THE GREAT CHOCOLATE PYRAMID

▲ John & Shari Rudy ▲

BRUNDAGE PUBLISHING

THE GREAT CHOCOLATE PYRAMID
by

John & Shari Rudy

BRUNDAGE PUBLISHING
Room 203 Executive Office Building
33 West State Street
Binghamton, NY 13901

www.BrundagePublishing.com

Front cover by Ruben Acevedo and John Rudy
Back cover and jacket layout by Angela Capria
Interior cartoons by John Rudy and Lewis Agrell

Edited by Rachel Edwards

Library of Congress
Control Number: 2005934077

ISBN Number: 1-892451-40-9

Printed in the United States of America

This book is dedicated to

♠ J.C. AND TYLER ♠

It is also dedicated to the memory of Grandma Gossner and her store, *The Chocolate Tree*.

TABLE OF CONTENTS

INTRODUCTION

I have been fascinated with chocolate all of my life. Some of my earliest and fondest memories are of time spent at my grandmother's store, *The Chocolate Tree*. She had chocolate gifts, chocolate ice cream cones and lots of yummy chocolate candies. Thank goodness she was a perfectionist, because any time chocolates at her store had even the slightest imperfections, she would get rid of them. Her disposal method was to put them in five-pound boxes and give them to our family. Our family favorites included the English toffees, chocolate turtles and milk chocolate butter creams. At times we could have three or more of these five-pound boxes at home, so we would traipse around the neighborhood spreading goodwill (chocolate) to our friends. At night, I would dream about working in that store when I became old enough. She sold the store before I reached working age, but this minor setback never discouraged my love for chocolate. As I grew up, I pondered life's difficult questions: *If I eat equal amounts of dark chocolate and white chocolate, is that a balanced diet? Has anyone ever spent a chocolate coin? Some people are interested in how to store chocolate. Why?*

Life is full of important questions, and choosing what to eat is one of the most critical ones. Each year you consume about 1,000 meals, and each time you eat you are faced with choices about what to eat. Over time, the choices of what you eat will affect your body and your mind. By learning the Chocolate Food Pyramid, you can choose tempting tastes and make delicious decisions—faster than you can say, "Bon-Bon."

In this book, you will find ways to eat chocolate at every meal while maintaining the recommended servings from each food group. Meals no longer need to be boring…they can be sweet and satisfying. I trust you will enjoy reading this book as much as I enjoyed eating the chocolate while writing it.

♠ John

For additional information, visit thechocolatepyramid.com.

USING THIS BOOK

Recipes:

In this book, you will find more than eighty irresistible chocolate recipes to drive your taste buds wild. There are six food groupings on the chocolate pyramid: Bread & Cereal Group, Vegetable Group, Fruit Group, Milk Group, Meat Group, and Fats & Sweets Group. For each of these food groupings, there are ten wickedly delightful recipes. If you are one of those chocoholics who must have their chocolate now, a "Quick Fix" section is included with twenty fast and easy recipes just for you.

Each recipe throughout the book has a difficulty rating assigned to it. This rating will give you some guidance concerning the difficulty and time required to prepare the recipe. On a scale of one to five chips (▲), one chip means the recipe is extremely easy to make and five chips means it requires more culinary expertise.

The author has selected his favorite recipe in each section. You will find a star (*) next to the recipe name.

Techniques for Melting Chocolate:

A lot of recipes in this book call for melted chocolate, so it is important to understand how to melt chocolate without scorching it. When chocolate scorches, it becomes grainy and bitter. Chocolate can scorch easily, so it is best not to melt it over direct heat unless it is mixed with other ingredients. It is also important to keep in mind that chocolate melts from the inside out, so though it may appear solid, upon stirring it will transform into a liquid. It is recommended to use a rubber spatula for stirring.

Stovetop: Melt chocolate in a double-boiler. If you do not have one, it is easy to make your own. Place the chocolate in a stainless-steel mixing bowl. On the stovetop, place a 2-quart saucepan filled with 1½ inches of water. Bring water to a boil and turn off heat. Cut chocolate into small pieces and place in mixing bowl. Place bowl over hot water so it rests on top of the saucepan, making a double boiler. The water should not be touching the bottom of the bowl. Stir chocolate until melted and smooth.

Microwave: Cut chocolate into small pieces and place in microwave-safe bowl. Heat on medium 30 seconds. You may microwave larger quantities on high. Remove from microwave and stir. Repeat until chocolate is melted.

Oven: To melt large quantities, cut into small pieces and drop into roasting pan. Place pan in oven at lowest temperature setting. Test chocolate every five minutes to see if melted. If you have plenty of time, place pan in oven with a pilot light and let sit. The chocolate will melt slowly and evenly over several hours.

Special Features:

Delicious Declarations: Many have made memorable comments about chocolate throughout the years. In this feature, you will hear statements that some famous (and some not-so-famous) people have made about chocolate.

Heavenly Humor: Enjoy some delectable cartoons and humorous quips in this feature. While most of the world has a love affair with chocolate, there is plenty of room to laugh at and have fun with it.

Tantalizing Tidbits: Enhance your chocolate IQ with note-worthy facts and interesting trivia. Learn some of the reasons why this sweet treat has come to be known as one of the greatest treasures ever discovered.

Chocolate Challenge: Do you know all there is to know about chocolate? Test your prowess with the fun quizzes throughout this book.

CHOCOLATE TYPES

Unsweetened Chocolate is the cooled and hardened version of 100% chocolate liquor. Sometimes it is referred to as baking or bitter chocolate. This chocolate is most often used in recipes, since it does not taste very good by itself.

Dark/Sweet Chocolate is a combination of cocoa solids, cocoa butter and sugar. While it must contain a minimum of 15% chocolate liquor, higher quality chocolates can have substantially more. It also has a higher sugar level than semi-sweet chocolate.

Semi-sweet/Bittersweet Chocolate must contain at least 35% chocolate liquor. Though available in bars, this chocolate is most often found in baking chips. European companies label this chocolate as bittersweet or dark, while American companies refer to this chocolate as semi-sweet. In general, bittersweet chocolates carry a stronger chocolate flavor due to unsweetened chocolate content of 50% or more, while semi-sweet chocolate generally contains 35–45% unsweetened chocolate.

Milk Chocolate is America's favorite chocolate. It contains at least 10% chocolate liquor and 12% milk solids. Mass-marketed milk chocolate can often have a sugar content as high as 50%. Due to its milk content, it is intolerant to heat and therefore difficult to cook and bake with.

White Chocolate is made from cocoa butter, sugar, milk and vanilla; the same ingredients as milk chocolate, but without the chocolate liquor. This is the sweetest and perhaps the most fragile form of all the chocolates, so pay close attention to it while heating or melting. There currently is no Standard of Identity for white chocolate.

Couverture is high-quality chocolate used by professional chefs for dipping, coating, molding and baking. Due to a minimum of 32% cocoa solids, this chocolate becomes very fluid when melted, providing the perfect coating to dipped truffles and candies. "Couverture" is French for "covering."

Ganache is a blend of dark chocolate and crème, and is a thick and extremely rich chocolate spread. It is commonly used between the layers of gourmet chocolate cakes.

Decorator's/Confectioner's Chocolate is not really chocolate at all. This chocolate-flavored candy is used for things such as covering strawberries. It melts easily and hardens quickly, but is *not* chocolate. If you want quick and easy, use decorator's chocolate; if you want perfection, use real chocolate and patience.

Cocoa is chocolate liquor with much of the cocoa butter removed. Store in a cool, dry place since it can pick up moisture and odors from other products in your kitchen.

    Nonalkalized cocoa is light in color and somewhat acidic with a strong chocolate flavor. Use this cocoa in recipes that call for baking soda; it will create a leavening action that causes the batter to rise when placed in the oven.

    Dutch process/Alkalized cocoa is cocoa that has been specially treated with an alkali to neutralize the natural acids in the chocolate. It is darker and milder in taste than nonalkalized cocoa. Since it is neutral and does not react with baking soda, it needs to be used in recipes calling for baking powder. If you do not have alkalized cocoa powder and must substitute nonalkalized, simply add a dash of baking soda to the cocoa.

The Standards of Identity govern the names and composition of chocolate and cocoa products in the United States. These standards were created by the Food and Drug Administration (FDA) and set the required percentages for key ingredients in these products. The first FDA standards were established December 6, 1944 and updated in the 1990s. The Codex Commission is currently working to unify US and European chocolate and cocoa standards.

THE GREAT CHOCOLATE PYRAMID

▲ ▲ ▲

GRAINS

- ♠ Banana Bread
- ♠ Biscotti*
- ♠ Breakfast Bars
- ♠ Buttermilk Pancakes
- ♠ Cranberry Scones
- ♠ Fruitcake
- ♠ Granola
- ♠ Nut Bread
- ♠ Pumpkin Bread
- ♠ Zucchini Muffins

CHOCOLATE CHIP BANANA BREAD

Difficulty: ♠ ♠ ♠
Preparation Time: 30 minutes
Yield: 1 loaf

1 cup all-purpose flour
½ cup whole wheat flour
1 teaspoon baking soda
1 teaspoon baking powder
⅛ teaspoon salt
¾ cup semi-sweet chocolate chips
½ cup walnuts or other nut, chopped
½ cup butter, softened
1 cup sugar
2 large eggs
1½ cups ripe bananas, mashed
1½ tablespoons lemon juice
2 teaspoons vanilla extract

1. Heat oven to 350°. Grease and flour bottom and sides of 9x5x3-inch loaf pan.

2. In medium bowl, mix flours, baking soda, baking powder and salt.

3. In small bowl, combine chocolate chips and walnuts.

4. In large bowl with electric mixer, cream butter and sugar until fluffy. Beat in eggs, mashed bananas, lemon juice and vanilla extract. Beat in dry mixture on low speed until blended.

5. Spoon one-third batter into loaf pan. Sprinkle half of chocolate chip mixture on top. Carefully spoon another one-third of batter over chocolate chip mixture. Sprinkle with remaining chocolate chip mixture. Spoon remaining batter over chocolate chip mixture.

6. Bake 65 minutes or until toothpick inserted into center comes out clean.

7. Cool in pan 10 minutes. Turn out onto rack and cool completely.

1. Good tasting techniques for dark chocolate include:
   a) Tasting on an empty stomach.
   b) Ensuring the chocolate's temperature is 66–77°F.
   c) Allowing chocolate to sit in mouth momentarily, so it can release primary flavors and aromas.
   d) Chewing it seven to ten times to release secondary aromas.
   e) All of the above

2. Under normal conditions (no extreme heat or moisture) what is the shelf life for chocolate?
   a) One month
   b) One year
   c) Five years
   d) Ten years

3. Which of the following types of chocolate is most commonly available for use in cooking?
   a) Dark chocolate
   b) Milk chocolate
   c) Unsweetened chocolate
   d) Cocoa

4. The ideal temperature for storing chocolate is 54–68°F. Fluctuating temperatures should be avoided as they will accelerate the appearance of:
   a) Sugarbloom
   b) Fatbloom
   c) Berrybloom
   d) Rightbloom

♠ *Solutions on page 140*

CHOCOLATE BISCOTTI

Difficulty: ♠ ♠ ♠
Preparation Time: 30 minutes
Yield: 24 biscotti

½ cup butter or margarine, softened
1¼ cups sugar
2 large eggs
¾ teaspoon vanilla
2 cups flour
⅓ cup cocoa
1½ teaspoons baking powder
½ teaspoon salt
¼ teaspoon almond extract
1 cup pecans or blanched almonds, finely chopped
1 cup semi-sweet chocolate chips

1. Heat oven to 325°.

2. In large bowl with electric mixer, cream butter and sugar. Beat in eggs, vanilla and almond extract.

3. In medium bowl, combine flour, cocoa, baking powder and salt. Add dry mixture to butter mixture. Mix in finely chopped pecans and chocolate chips.

4. On waxed paper or cutting board, shape dough into 2 logs two inches wide and twelve inches long. Place on ungreased cookie sheet three inches apart.

5. Bake 45–50 minutes.

6. Cool slightly and cut in half-inch diagonal slices.

7. Bake 30 minutes.

8. Cool on wire rack.

♠ What do you get when you cross an alligator with a Hershey's bar?
Answer: Chocodile.

CHOCOLATE BREAKFAST BARS

Difficulty: ♠ ♠
Preparation Time: 20 minutes
Yield: 18 bars

3 ounces white chocolate
1½ cups honey
4 tablespoons butter
1 tablespoon vanilla
5 cups oats
1 cup pecans or your favorite nut
1 cup dried cherries (you can substitute other dried fruit)
½ cup shredded coconut
⅔ cup crunchy peanut butter

1. In 4-quart saucepan, melt chocolate, honey and butter. Boil 1 minute. Remove from heat and add vanilla.

2. In large bowl, mix together remaining ingredients. Stir into chocolate mixture.

3. Pour dough onto greased and floured cookie sheet. Smooth into a large rectangle about one-inch thick.

4. Cool before serving.

♠ When tasting chocolate, make sure your palette is completely clean. Place the chocolate on your tongue, then slowly move it around your mouth. Chocoholics will tell you that a quality chocolate's taste will gradually hit you and then linger for a while. If the taste quickly disappears, it is poor quality chocolate. If the bar or box of chocolate quickly disappears, it was good chocolate!

CHOCOLATE CHIP BUTTERMILK PANCAKES

Difficulty: ♠ ♠
Preparation Time: 10 minutes
Yield: 14 pancakes

2 cups flour
2 teaspoons baking powder
1 teaspoon baking soda
3 tablespoons sugar
½ teaspoon salt
2 large eggs
2 cups buttermilk
½ cup chocolate chips, reserved

1. Heat griddle to 375°.

2. In medium bowl, combine dry ingredients and mix well.

3. In large bowl, beat eggs slightly with a fork. Add buttermilk and stir until combined.

4. Add dry ingredients to egg mixture and stir with wooden spoon until just combined. Do not over mix.

5. Spoon ¼ cup batter onto griddle for each pancake.

6. Immediately distribute desired amount of chocolate chips into batter of each pancake before they cook. (I choose not to add the chips to the batter since they tend to sink to the bottom and I want to ensure each pancake gets its fair share of chocolate.)

7. When edge of pancakes begin to harden (the bubbles that form in the batter no longer disappear), flip pancakes. Cook 1 minute and serve immediately.

TANTALIZING Tidbits

♠ Italians prefer their chocolate mixed with almonds, hazelnuts, and chestnuts.

♠ The largest consumers of chocolate in Europe are the Germans.

♠ Belgium is well-known for their chocolate-covered pralines, called *ballotins*. Their most recognizable chocolate company is Godiva.

♠ Dark, intensely flavored chocolate is the choice of the French. Innovative efforts by French chocolatiers have led to chocolate being celebrated as an object of artistic skill and culinary refinement.

♠ In Mexico, chocolate is still preferred as a beverage. *Mole* (pronounced mo-lay) comes from the Nahuatl word *Mulli* which means "sauce." Moles are savory sauces often used in Mexican cooking that feature chocolate as a key ingredient.

♠ You would not have much success in China selling chocolate in a blue wrapper, because the Chinese associate blue with death.

♠ Americans eat approximately ten pounds of chocolate per year per capita. The Swiss eat roughly twenty-two pounds per year and consume more chocolate per capita than any other nation on earth.

♠ Research shows that Venezuela produced half of the world's chocolate by 1810, and one-third of that was consumed by the Spaniards.

WHITE CHOCOLATE CRANBERRY SCONES

Difficulty: ♠ ♠ ♠
Preparation Time: 25 minutes
Yield: 18 scones

2½ cups all-purpose flour
¾ cup whole wheat flour
¾ cup granulated sugar
¾ teaspoon salt
1 teaspoon baking soda
2½ teaspoons baking powder
2½ cups oats
1 cup dried cranberries, roughly chopped (or other dried fruit)
1¼ cups unsalted butter, room temperature
¾ cup buttermilk
1 cup white chocolate chips

Glaze:
2 tablespoons heavy cream
2 tablespoons granulated sugar

1. Combine all dry ingredients in bowl of an electric mixer. Add cranberries and mix with paddle attachment. Add butter and mix on low speed until mixture resembles coarse meal. Add white chocolate chips and buttermilk. Mix until just combined.

2. Turn dough out onto a lightly floured surface. With hands, work mixture into three rounds, half-inch high and nine inches wide. Score each round into six pie wedges. Cover with plastic wrap and freeze 2 hours.

3. Heat oven to 350º.

4. Remove dough from freezer and cut pie wedges with sharp knife. Place scones one inch apart on greased and floured cookie sheet.

5. Bake 5 minutes. Remove from oven.

Glaze:

6. Brush scones with heavy cream and sprinkle with sugar. Bake 12 minutes or until lightly golden.

7. Cool before serving.

DELICIOUS Declarations!

The divine drink, which builds up resistance and fights fatigue. A cup of this precious drink (cocoa) permits a man to walk for a whole day without food.
♠ Montezuma, Aztec Emperor (c. 1480–1520)

If you are not feeling well, if you have not slept, chocolate will revive you. But you have no chocolate! I think of that again and again! My dear, how will you ever manage?
♠ Marquise de Sevigne, 1677

Chocolate is a perfect food, as wholesome as it is delicious, a beneficent restorer of exhausted power. It is the best friend of those engaged in literary pursuits.
♠ Baron Justus von Liebig (1803–1873), Chemist

Diet tip: Eat a chocolate bar before each meal; it'll take the edge off of your appetite, and you'll eat less.
♠ Unknown, *The Rules of Chocolate*

If one swallows a cup of chocolate only three hours after a copious lunch, everything will be perfectly digested and there will still be room for dinner.
♠ Brillat-Savarin

The cocoa bean is a phenomenon, for nowhere else has nature concentrated such a wealth of valuable nourishment in so small a space.
♠ Alexander von Humboldt, German Scientist

The beverage of the gods was Ambrosia; that of man is chocolate. Both increase the length of life in a prodigious manner.
♠ Louis Lewin, MD, *Phantastica*

FRUITCAKE

Difficulty: ♠♠♠♠
Preparation Time: 45 minutes
Yield: 44 bars

2 cups raisins
3 cups water
½ cup shortening
2 cups sugar
1 teaspoon nutmeg
1 teaspoon ground cloves
1 teaspoon cinnamon
1 tablespoon cocoa
1 tablespoon baking soda
1 cup dates, chopped
1 cup walnuts or pecans, chopped
1 cup orange juice
Grated rind of one orange
½ cup diced maraschino cherries
5 cups flour

1. Heat oven to 325°. Grease and flour baking pans. I like to use a 13x9x2-inch pan and an 8x8x2-inch pan. You may wish to use loaf pans instead.

2. In 3-quart saucepan, boil raisins and 2 cups water until raisins are tender. Remove from heat. Add shortening and stir until melted. Add 1 cup cold water and cool.

3. Beat in remaining ingredients until well mixed. Pour into pans.

4. Bake 1 hour or until toothpick inserted into center comes out clean and mixture begins to pull away from sides of pan.

5. Cool and serve.

GRANOLA

Difficulty: ♠ ♠
Preparation time: 12 minutes
Yield: 8 servings

4 cups oats
1 cup wheat germ
½ cup chopped walnuts or slivered almonds
¼ cup brown sugar
1 teaspoon cinnamon
¼ teaspoon salt
¼ cup vegetable oil
⅓ cup honey
⅓ cup water
½ cup sweetened dried cranberries or raisins
⅓ cup semi-sweet chocolate chips

1. Heat oven to 300°.

2. In large mixing bowl, stir together oats, wheat germ, nuts, brown sugar, cinnamon and salt. Slowly add oil, honey and water. Mix thoroughly.

3. Spread mixture evenly on a deep cookie sheet.

4. Bake 40 minutes or until lightly browned, turning mixture over every 10 minutes to prevent burning.

5. When done, remove from oven and cool completely.

6. Mix in cranberries and chocolate chips, and serve.

♠ Seven days without chocolate makes one weak.

♠ I am not overweight—I am chocolate-enriched.

_____ 1. More than 100 billion M&M's are produced each year at the Mars M&M's factory in Hackettstown, New Jersey.

_____ 2. The Tootsie Roll was invented in 1931.

_____ 3. The Curtis Candy Company named the Baby Ruth candy bar in honor of the great baseball player Babe Ruth.

_____ 4. Forrest Mars Sr. invented the recipe for M&M's during World War I.

_____ 5. Hershey's makes 100 million chocolate Kisses every day.

_____ 6. The Hershey's Chocolate Bar is the most popular candy bar in the United States.

_____ 7. The official state cookie of Massachusetts is the chocolate chip cookie.

_____ 8. Most Americans prefer dark chocolate.

_____ 9. In the United States, chocolate candy outsells all other types of candy combined.

_____ 10. Consumers spend more than $7 billion a year on chocolate.

♠ *Solutions on page 140*

CHOCOLATE NUT BREAD

Difficulty: ♠ ♠
Preparation time: 20 minutes
Yield: 2 loaves

3 ounces unsweetened chocolate
½ cup butter or margarine, softened
3 cups flour
1 teaspoon baking powder
½ teaspoon baking soda
1 teaspoon salt
1 cup sugar
2 large eggs
1 cup milk
1 tablespoon vanilla extract
⅓ cup pecans or walnuts, chopped

1. Heat oven to 350°. Grease and flour two 9x5x3-inch loaf pans.

2. In 2-quart saucepan over low heat, stir together chocolate and butter until melted. Remove from heat and set aside.

3. In medium bowl, mix together dry ingredients.

4. In large bowl with electric mixer, beat eggs, milk, vanilla and pecans.

5. Alternately add dry mixture and chocolate mixture to egg mixture. Beat until smooth. Pour batter into pans.

6. Bake 45 minutes or until toothpick inserted into center comes out clean.

7. Cool 10 minutes, then remove from pans and cool completely on wire racks.

DELICIOUS Declarations!

A true chocolate lover finds ways to accommodate his passion and make it work with his lifestyle.
♠ Julie Davis, *The Los Angeles Times*

I never met a chocolate I didn't like.
♠ Deanna Troi, *Star Trek: The Next Generation*

Nine out of ten people like chocolate—the tenth person always lies.
♠ John Q. Tullius

What you see before you, my friend, is the result of a lifetime of chocolate.
♠ Katharine Hepburn

What use are cartridges in battle? I always carry chocolate instead.
♠ George Bernard Shaw

Nevermind about 1066 William the Conqueror, 1087 William the Second. Such things are not going to affect one's life…but 1932 the Mars Bar and 1936 Maltesers and 1937 the Kit Kat—these dates are milestones in history and should be seared into the memory of every child in the country.
♠ Roald Dahl

Always serve too much hot fudge sauce on hot fudge sundaes. It makes people overjoyed, and puts them in your debt.
♠ Judith Olney

IT'S THE ONLY PLACE SECURE ENOUGH
TO STORE MY CHOCOLATE!

CHOCOLATE CHIP PUMPKIN BREAD

Difficulty: ♠ ♠
Preparation Time: 20 minutes
Yield: 1 loaf

⅓ cup butter or margarine
1 cup sugar
2 large eggs
1¼ cups canned pumpkin filling
2 cups flour
1 teaspoon baking soda
1 teaspoon cinnamon
½ teaspoon nutmeg
1 teaspoon pumpkin pie spice
¼ teaspoon ground cloves
¼ teaspoon ground ginger
¼ cup chocolate chips
⅓ cup walnuts, chopped

Topping:
1 tablespoon heavy cream
½ cup powdered sugar

1. Heat oven to 350°. Grease and flour bottom and sides of 9x5x3-inch loaf pan.

2. In large bowl with electric mixer, cream butter. Gradually add sugar, vanilla, eggs and pumpkin. Mix well.

3. In medium bowl, combine flour, baking soda, cinnamon, nutmeg, pumpkin spice, cloves, and ginger. Stir into wet mixture, blending well. Stir in chocolate chips and nuts. Pour batter into prepared pan.

4. Bake 45–50 minutes or until toothpick inserted into center comes out clean.

5. Cool on wire rack. Remove from loaf pan.

Topping:

6. In small bowl, stir together cream and powdered sugar. Spread over top and sides of bread with knife.

ZUCCHINI MUFFINS

Difficulty: ♠ ♠ ♠
Preparation Time: 25 minutes
Yield: 24 muffins

3 large eggs
2 cups sugar
1 cup vegetable oil
⅓ cup unsweetened cocoa
1½ teaspoons vanilla
2 cups zucchini, grated
1 teaspoon baking soda
½ teaspoon baking powder
3 cups flour
1 teaspoon salt
¼ teaspoon ground cinnamon
¼ teaspoon ground nutmeg
¼ teaspoon ground cloves
1 teaspoon pumpkin pie spice

1. Heat oven to 350º. Grease or line 2 12-cup muffin tins with paper liners.

2. In large bowl, beat eggs, sugar and oil. Add cocoa, vanilla and zucchini and stir.

3. In large bowl, whisk together remaining ingredients.

4. Pour dry ingredients into chocolate zucchini mixture and stir well. Pour batter into prepared muffin tins filling each cup two-thirds full.

5. Bake 22–25 minutes.

6. Cool before serving.

♠ Letter from college student to parents: *Things are bad. Send chocolate!*

TANTALIZING
Tidbits

♠ Cocoa trees are very delicate and sensitive plants, and require protection from the wind and the sun. Cocoa seedlings are planted in fiber baskets or plastic bags in nurseries. After a few months they are transplanted in their container. Other trees are used to shade newly-planted seedlings; these trees are called "cocoa mothers."

♠ *Cacao* or *cocoa*? Both are correct, it just depends on what you are talking about. Cacao is the botanical name for the Cacao tree, as well as its pods and unfermented beans. Perhaps due to a spelling mistake by English importers, beans from the cacao tree became known as cocoa beans in English speaking countries. Cocoa describes the dry powder, liquor, and fermented beans that become chocolate.

♠ The cocoa tree, *Theobroma cocoa*, grows a brownish-yellow to purplish fruit. This fruit has a whitish pulp, and holds twenty to forty dark seeds in each pod. When these seeds are dried and processed, they are known as "cocoa beans."

♠ In 1822, Ferreira Gomes from Portugal introduced the cocoa tree as an ornamental plant off the west coast of Africa on the Principe Island in the Gulf of Guinea.

♠ The New York Cocoa Exchange was formed in 1925. It was started so that buyers and sellers of chocolate could get together for transactions.

♠ Cacao beans have been used as a form of currency in various parts of the world. The Aztec empire used cacao beans for currency. A 1545 document stated that the average wage of a porter in Central Mexico was 100 beans per day; these beans could be traded for other commodities. One cacao bean would purchase one large tomato, five green chilies, or one tamale. Three beans would purchase a turkey egg, while thirty beans would purchase one small rabbit.

VEGETABLES

- Beet Brownies*
- Carrot Cake
- Mashed Potato Cake
- Onion Cookies
- Pumpkin Cookies
- Sauerkraut Cake
- Spinach Soup
- Stuffed Celery
- White Chocolate Onions
- Zucchini Nut Loaf

BEET CHOCOLATE BROWNIES

Difficulty: ♠ ♠ ♠
Preparation Time: 25 minutes
Yield: 28 brownies

½ cup butter or margarine
4 ounces unsweetened chocolate
4 large eggs
1 cup brown sugar, firmly packed
1 cup applesauce
1 teaspoon vanilla
1½ cups flour
½ teaspoon salt
½ teaspoon nutmeg
1 teaspoon cinnamon
1 teaspoon baking powder
15 ounces beets packed in water, drained and mashed
½ cup almonds or other nut, finely chopped
½ cup whole wheat flour

1. Heat oven to 350º. Grease bottom and sides of 13x9x2-inch pan.

2. In 2-quart saucepan, melt butter and chocolate over low heat. Set aside to cool.

3. In large bowl with electric mixer, beat eggs 2 minutes. Add sugar and vanilla and continue beating until well combined. Stir in chocolate mixture, applesauce and beets.

4. In large bowl, sift together flour, salt, spices and baking powder. Stir into chocolate mixture. Fold in wheat flour and almonds. Spoon batter into prepared pan.

5. Bake 32 minutes or until toothpick inserted into center comes out clean.

6. Cool 15 minutes and serve warm.

♠ How much are you willing to pay for chocolate? Godiva recently launched their G Collection to rave reviews, and a big price tag—$100 per pound.

♠ The Whitman's Sampler is the best-selling box of chocolates in the United States. It was introduced to the market in 1912.

♠ The Butterfinger candy bar was first produced by Chicago's Curtis Candy Company in 1923. As an advertising ploy, candy bars were dropped from an airplane on cities in forty states.

♠ In the 2002 global vote, purple became the newest member of the M&M's family. Pink and turquoise were its competitors.

♠ Yoo-Hoo is a chocolate-flavored soft drink that was invented in the 1920s by Mr. Natale Olivieri.

♠ Nutella spread is a creamy, chocolaty hazelnut spread. It was created in the 1940s by Pietro Ferrero, a pastry maker and founder of the Ferrero Company. At the time, cocoa was in short supply due to war rationing. Chocolate was an expensive delicacy, so Pietro mixed cocoa with toasted hazelnuts, cocoa butter and vegetable oils to create an economical chocolate spread. Today, Nutella is the #1 spread in Europe. Worldwide, it outsells all brands of peanut butter combined.

♠ Samuel Adams, Boston Beer Company, offered a limited edition Chocolate Bock in 2004 for Valentine's Day. 50,000 wine-sized bottles of beer were produced.

♠ Toblerone bars have a triangular profile representing the Swiss Alps.

CHOCOLATE CARROT CAKE

Difficulty: ♠ ♠ ♠ ♠
Preparation Time: 45 minutes
Yield: 8 servings

1½ cups finely grated carrots
¾ cup granulated sugar
½ cup vegetable oil
1 cup boiling water
1 cup flour
½ cup whole wheat flour
½ cup cocoa
1 tablespoon cinnamon
¼ teaspoon nutmeg
½ teaspoon salt
1½ teaspoons baking powder
½ cup semi-sweet chocolate chips

Frosting:
¼ cup butter, softened
6 ounces cream cheese
⅓ teaspoon vanilla
¾ teaspoon grated orange peel
1½ cups powdered sugar, sifted
2 tablespoons low-fat milk

1. Heat oven to 350°. Grease bottom and sides of 8x8x2-inch pan.

2. In large bowl, combine carrots, sugar and oil. Pour water over mixture.

3. In medium bowl, combine rest of the ingredients. Add to carrot mixture and mix well. Pour into pan.

4. Bake 35 minutes.

5. Cool.

Frosting:

6. In medium bowl, combine ingredients and beat well.

7. Spread evenly on top of cake.

1. One chocolate chip provides enough food energy for an adult to walk:
   a) 3 feet
   b) 15 feet
   c) 100 feet
   d) 150 feet

2. Approximately how many chocolate chips would you need to eat to generate sufficient food energy for a hike around the world?
   a) 750,000
   b) 875,000
   c) 1,000,000
   d) 1,125,000

3. Which food has the highest level of antioxidants?
   a) White chocolate
   b) Raisins
   c) Oranges
   d) Dark chocolate

♠ *Solutions on page 141*

MASHED POTATO CHOCOLATE CAKE

This recipe is a joy to make when you have leftover mashed potatoes. This cuts preparation time by about 35 minutes.

Difficulty: ♠ ♠ ♠
Preparation Time: 60 minutes
Yield: 32 bars

1 cup margarine or butter
2 cups granulated sugar
4 large eggs
3 ounces dark chocolate, melted
1½ teaspoons vanilla
1 cup cold mashed potatoes (2 medium potatoes)
1 teaspoon baking soda
2 cups flour
1 teaspoon salt
¾ cup buttermilk

1. Heat oven to 375°. Grease and flour bottom and sides of 13x9x2-inch pan.

2. In large bowl with electric mixer, cream together butter and sugar. One at a time, beat in eggs. Stir in melted chocolate, vanilla and potatoes.

3. In medium bowl, combine flour, baking soda and salt. Pour into potato mixture.

4. Add buttermilk and mix well. Spread into pan.

5. Bake 45 minutes.

6. Cool and serve.

If needed, directions to make mashed potatoes: Quarter, peal and boil potatoes in 4-quart saucepan until potatoes easily separate when poked with a fork. Mash potatoes with ½ cup milk and heaping teaspoon of butter. Chill potatoes 15 minutes before combining in recipe.

ONION CHOCOLATE CHIP COOKIES

Difficulty: ♠ ♠ ♠
Preparation Time: 20 minutes
Yield: 32 cookies

1 cup butter or margarine, softened
¾ cup brown sugar
¾ cup granulated sugar
2 large eggs
1 teaspoon vanilla
2½ cups flour
1 teaspoon baking soda
1 teaspoon salt
1½ cups semi-sweet chocolate chips
¾ cup sweet onion, minced

1.   Heat oven to 375°. Grease two cookie sheets.

2.   In large bowl with electric mixer, cream together butter, brown sugar and granulated sugar. With electric mixer, beat in eggs and vanilla.

3.   In medium bowl, combine flour, baking soda and salt. Add to batter and stir well.

4.   Stir in chocolate chips.

5.   Spoon by heaping teaspoonfuls onto cookie sheets about two inches apart. Using the back of a spoon, gently flatten cookie dough and sprinkle onions on top.

6.   Bake 12–14 minutes or until golden brown.

7.   Remove from oven and serve warm.

♠ You can substitute cocoa for unsweetened or semi-sweet baking chocolate in a recipe, except in coatings, puddings, or pie fillings.

CHOCOLATE Challenge

_____ 1. In Hershey, Pennsylvania the street lights on the main street are shaped like Hershey's Kisses.

_____ 2. The Chocolate Mountains can be found in Imperial County, California.

_____ 3. You can find the word "chocoholic" defined in the dictionary.

_____ 4. Chocolate was exclusively for drinking until the early Victorian era.

_____ 5. In some parts of Central America, cocoa beans were used as currency as recently as the 19th century.

_____ 6. Back in the 16th century, French physicians considered chocolate to be an aphrodisiac.

_____ 7. Chocolaterias (chocolate houses) are still common in Spain today.

_____ 8. Beautifully designed chocolate boxes became fashionable in France as early as 1880.

♠ _Solutions on page 141_

PUMPKIN COOKIES

Difficulty: ♠♠
Preparation Time: 20 minutes
Yield: 44 cookies

1½ cups butter
2 cups brown sugar
1 large egg
2 teaspoons vanilla extract
2 cups pumpkin filling
4 cups flour
2 cups rolled oats
2 teaspoons baking soda
2 teaspoons cinnamon
1 teaspoon salt
1¼ cups chocolate chips
½ cup walnuts or other nut, chopped
Powdered sugar (optional)

1. Heat oven to 325°. Grease cookie sheet.

2. In large bowl with electric mixer, cream butter, sugar, egg, vanilla and pumpkin. Beat until light and fluffy. Mix in dry ingredients.

3. Drop on cookie sheets by tablespoonfuls. Leave 1½ inches between cookies as they will spread out.

4. Bake 22 minutes or until firm and lightly golden brown.

5. Remove from oven and dust with powdered sugar before serving.

♠ Friend to friend:
Mike: "You can have my M&M's."
Bill: "You don't like candy?"
Mike: "Not this kind. They are too hard to peel."

TANTALIZING Tidbits

♠ Chocolate readily absorbs other flavors and odors, so do not store it near chemicals, perfumes, or foods with a strong aroma.

♠ Quality chocolate should snap crisply when a piece is broken off. It is too dry if it splinters and too waxy if it bends before breaking.

♠ Chocolate has over 500 flavor components; more than twice the amount found in strawberry and vanilla.

♠ The finest filled chocolates, such as truffles, normally have a shelf life of roughly ten to fourteen days when stored at room temperature. The short shelf life is due to the perishable qualities of the fresh creams and butters in the filling.

♠ Do not store chocolate near heat or in direct sunlight. Light causes color to fade, while hot temperatures cause tackiness and melting.

♠ In general, solid chocolate that is not mixed with other products will have a shelf life of at least six to twelve months or longer, depending on the environmental storage conditions. When mixed with other products (nuts, cream, etc.) the shelf life will be reduced.

♠ White chocolate is somewhat of a misnomer. In the United States, in order to be legally called "chocolate," a product must contain cocoa solids. White chocolate does not contain these solids, which leaves it the smooth ivory or beige color. Real white chocolate is primarily cocoa butter, sugar, milk, and vanilla. There are, however, some forms of white chocolate that are made with vegetable oils instead of cocoa butter. Check the labels to avoid these cheap imitations.

SAUERKRAUT CHOCOLATE CAKE

Difficulty: ♠ ♠
Preparation Time: 30 minutes
Yield: 12 servings

¾ cup sauerkraut
1½ cups granulated sugar
⅔ cup butter or margarine
3 large eggs
1¼ teaspoons vanilla
¼ teaspoon salt
½ cup cocoa
2¼ cups flour
1 teaspoon baking soda
1 teaspoon baking powder
1 cup water
Powdered sugar (optional)

1. Heat oven to 375º. Grease and flour 13x9x2-inch pan.

2. Chop, rinse and drain sauerkraut well.

3. In large bowl with electric mixer, cream butter and sugar well. Beat in eggs and vanilla.

4. In large bowl, sift together salt, cocoa, flour, baking soda and baking powder. Mix into batter, stirring in water when needed. Fold in sauerkraut and mix thoroughly. Pour batter into prepared pan.

5. Bake 35 minutes.

6. Cool and sprinkle with powdered sugar.

1. Ghirardelli's biggest contribution to the chocolate industry was the accidental discovery of a method for making:
   a) Virtually fat-free chocolate powder.
   b) White chocolate without any cacao solids.
   c) Chocolate that does not bloom when exposed to heat.
   d) Chocolate Easter eggs that contained a special gift.

2. Liqueur-filled chocolates were launched in 1987 in Las Vegas, Nevada at this company owned by Forrest Mars:
   a) Peter Paul
   b) Ethel M. Chocolates
   c) See's Candies
   d) Whitman's

3. Which of the following is true about Milton Hershey?
   a) He tried to develop onion and beet flavored sherbets.
   b) He made a fortune, but died penniless.
   c) He founded a home for orphaned boys in 1909.
   d) All of the above

4. Cadbury World can be found in which country?
   a) Netherlands
   b) Austria
   c) Great Britain
   d) Belgium

5. Which company offers organic chocolate?
   a) Jungle Chocolate
   b) Dagoba
   c) Newman's Own Organics
   d) Green & Black
   e) All of the above

♠ *Solutions on page 141*

SPINACH CHOCOLATE SOUP

Difficulty: ♠♠♠♠♠
Preparation Time: 90 minutes
Yield: 6 servings

1½ cups fresh spinach, chopped
5 tablespoons butter
4 large white mushrooms, diced
4 green onions, chopped
5 tablespoons flour
2 cups chicken broth
2 cups chocolate milk
½ teaspoon salt
½ teaspoon black pepper
4 ounces cream cheese, softened
1 cup Swiss cheese, grated

1. In 4-quart saucepan or 4-quart Dutch oven, melt butter. Sauté mushrooms and onions over medium heat until tender. Stir flour into vegetables and cook 2 minutes.

2. Whisk in chicken broth and milk. Stir until thickened.

3. Add salt, pepper, cream cheese and Swiss cheese. Stir until melted and creamy.

4. Add spinach. Stir gently and heat 10 minutes or until spinach is tender.

5. Season to taste and serve hot.

STUFFED CELERY

Difficulty: ♠
Preparation Time: 5 minutes
Yield: 12 pieces

6 celery stalks
½ cup peanut butter
⅛ cup semi-sweet chocolate chips

1. Wash, dry and cut celery stalks in half width-wise.

2. In small bowl, mix together peanut butter and chocolate chips.

3. Fill celery with peanut butter mixture.

4. Eat right away or chill 30 minutes and serve.

♠ Top Ten Reasons Why a Chocolate Kiss is Better Than a Kiss:

1. Chocolate is readily available.
2. Chocolate will not give you a cold.
3. Chocolate will not dry your lips.
4. You can eat chocolate in front of your parents.
5. Chocolate lasts longer.
6. You can have chocolate on the job.
7. Chocolate does not have bad breath.
8. You can have chocolate at any age.
9. Chocolate has no nose to get in the way.
10. You do not have to pucker.

WHITE CHOCOLATE ONIONS

Difficulty: ♠
Preparation Time: 35 minutes
Yield: 6 servings

5 tablespoons butter or margarine
⅛ teaspoon allspice
⅛ teaspoon ground cloves
⅛ teaspoon ground nutmeg
⅛ teaspoon ground red pepper
1 cup onion, cut lengthwise into slices ¼-inch wide
1 cup heavy cream
2 ounces white chocolate

1. In 3-quart saucepan, melt butter over low heat. Stir in allspice, cloves, red pepper and nutmeg. Add onion slices, and cover. Cook over low heat 10 minutes.

2. Stir and cook 10 more minutes.

3. Add cream and chocolate. Stir until chocolate melts.

4. Simmer 10 minutes.

5. Season to taste and serve warm.

DELICIOUS Declarations!

The taste of chocolate is a sensual pleasure in itself, existing in the same world as sex…For myself, I can enjoy the wicked pleasure of chocolate…entirely by myself.
♠ Dr. Ruth Westheimer

All I really need is love, but a little chocolate now and then doesn't hurt.
♠ Lucy Van Pelt, *Peanuts* by Charles M. Schulz

Don't wreck a sublime chocolate experience by feeling guilty. Chocolate isn't like sex. It will not make you pregnant, and it always feels good.
♠ Lora Brody, *Growing Up on the Chocolate Diet*

'Twill make old women young and fresh;
Create new motions of the flesh,
And cause them to long for you know what
If they but taste of chocolate.
♠ James Wadworth, *A History of the Nature and Quality of Chocolate*

Forget love—I'd rather fall in chocolate!
♠ Unknown

It's not that chocolates are a substitute for love—love is a substitute for chocolate. Chocolate is, let's face it, far more reliable than a man.
♠ Miranda Ingram

CHOCOLATE ZUCCHINI NUT LOAF

Difficulty: ♠ ♠ ♠
Preparation Time: 25 minutes
Yield: 2 loaves

2½ cups zucchini, grated (approximately 3 large zucchini)
3 large eggs
2 cups granulated sugar
1 cup vegetable oil
2 teaspoons vanilla
2 ounces unsweetened chocolate, melted
3 cups flour
½ teaspoon salt
1 teaspoon cinnamon
½ teaspoon baking powder
1 cup pecans or other nut, chopped

1. Heat oven to 350°. Lightly grease and flour 2 8½x4½x2½-inch loaf pans.

2. In medium bowl with electric mixer, beat eggs well. Beat in sugar, oil and vanilla. Stir in chocolate.

3. In large bowl, combine flour, salt, cinnamon and baking powder. Pour egg mixture over dry ingredients and stir thoroughly. Add nuts and zucchini. Pour half of batter into each prepared pan.

4. Bake 1 hour or until toothpick inserted into center comes out clean.

5. Cool completely before serving.

♠ A little boy was taken to the dentist. It was discovered that he had a cavity that would have to be filled.

"Now, young man," asked the dentist, "what kind of filling would you like for that tooth?"

"Chocolate, please," replied the youngster.

FRUITS

- Apricot Bundt Cake
- Apricot Torte
- Black Forest Coffee Cake
- Cherry Bread
- Chocolate Covered Strawberries and Bananas
- Coconut Chocolate Chip Cookies
- Figs and Dates
- Pear Cake*
- Pineapple Squares
- Tomato Soup Cake

CHOCOLATE APRICOT BUNDT CAKE

Difficulty: ♠ ♠ ♠
Preparation Time: 25 minutes
Yield: 12 servings

½ cup butter or margarine, softened
8 ounces cream cheese, softened
2½ cups sugar
½ cup unsweetened cocoa
5 large eggs
2½ cups cake flour
2 teaspoons baking powder
1 teaspoon baking soda
½ teaspoon salt
½ cup dried apricots, chopped
¾ cup semi-sweet chocolate chips

1. Heat oven to 350°. Grease 12-cup bundt cake pan.

2. In large bowl with electric mixer, beat together butter, cream cheese and 2 cups sugar. Add cocoa and eggs and beat well.

3. In medium bowl, combine cake flour, baking powder, baking soda and salt. Add to chocolate mixture. Beat with mixer on low until well blended.

4. In small bowl, combine ½ cup sugar, apricots and ⅔ of chocolate chips.

5. Spoon half of batter into bundt pan. Use back of wooden spoon to create a well around the center of batter. Add apricot mixture to center of ring, taking care to ensure mixture does not touch sides of pan. Spoon on remaining batter. Sprinkle remaining chocolate chips on top.

6. Bake 50 minutes or until toothpick inserted into center comes out clean.

7. Cool in pan 30 minutes. Invert onto plate and cool completely.

♠ Money can't buy you love, but it can buy you chocolate.

CHOCOLATE APRICOT TORTE

Difficulty: ♠ ♠ ♠
Preparation Time: 30 minutes
Yield: 9 servings

6 large eggs
¾ cup sugar
1 teaspoon vanilla extract
½ cup flour, sifted
¼ cup unsweetened cocoa, sifted
2 teaspoons ground cinnamon
1 teaspoon ground nutmeg
1 teaspoon pumpkin pie spice

Frosting and filling:
1 cup apricot all-fruit spread
2 cups dark chocolate frosting
1 tablespoon dry espresso (optional)
Fresh strawberries (optional)

1. Heat oven to 350°. Grease 2 8x1½-inch round cake pans.

2. In large bowl with electric mixer, beat eggs, sugar, and vanilla on high 8 minutes.

3. In medium bowl, sift together flour, cocoa powder, cinnamon, nutmeg and pumpkin pie spice. Fold dry ingredients into egg mixture and stir until well-combined. Pour half of mixture into each prepared pan.

4. Bake 18 minutes or until toothpick inserted into center comes out clean.

5. Cool completely.

6. When cool, remove cakes from pans. Using dental floss or cake separator, carefully split each layer in half horizontally. Remove top half of each layer and spread bottom half with apricot spread. Replace top half. You now have two cakes.

7. Place one cake on a plate and spread chocolate frosting on top. Stack second cake on top of first cake. Spread remaining frosting over top and sides of cake. Garnish with fresh strawberries.

TANTALIZING Tidbits

♠ Alfred Hitchcock used chocolate syrup to simulate blood in the famous shower scene of his 1960 black-and-white thriller, *Psycho*.

♠ In the movie *E.T.: The Extra-Terrestrial*, the script called for the boy Elliott to leave a trail of M&M's for E.T. to follow. Mars, the maker of M&M's, thought the film would be flop and said no to partnering for the film. When Hershey's Foods was approached, they eagerly agreed to have E.T. follow a path of Reese's Pieces.

♠ Learn mathematics with chocolate with tasty titles such as *The Hershey's Milk Chocolate Multiplication Book, Hershey's Fraction Book and Game Pack*, and *The M&M's Brand Chocolate Candies Counting Board Book*.

♠ Here are some "chocolaty" movie titles. Can you think of any more?
> *Willy Wonka and the Chocolate Factory*
> *Like Water for Chocolate*
> *Chocolat*
> *Better Than Chocolate*

♠ Peter Ostrum was the thirteen-year-old child actor who charmingly played Charlie in *Willy Wonka and the Chocolate Factory* (1971). He left the film industry directly after making the movie, which was his first and only film.

♠ Chocolate is so well loved that thousands of books have been written about the subject. Here are a few interesting titles:
> *Chocolate Fever*
> *Chocolate Therapy: Dare to Discover Your Inner Center!*
> *Chocolate Legs: Sweet Mother Savage Killer?*
> *Dying for Chocolate*

BLACK FOREST COFFEE CAKE

Difficulty: ♠ ♠
Preparation Time: 25 minutes
Yield: 12 servings

3 large eggs
1½ cups sugar
½ cup shortening
1½ cups milk
2 tablespoons vanilla
3 cups flour
2 tablespoons baking powder
1 cup chocolate chips
1 can cherry pie filling

Topping:
1 cup biscuit mix
½ cup sugar
¼ cup butter or margarine
½ cup chocolate chips
½ cup finely chopped pecans (optional)

1. Heat oven to 375°. Grease bottom and sides of 13x9x2-inch pan.

2. In large bowl with electric mixer, beat eggs. Mix in sugar, shortening, milk and vanilla. Add flour and baking powder. When well mixed, add chocolate chips. Pour into prepared pan.

3. Spoon cherry pie filling by the teaspoon in even rows (like the stripes on a flag) into the batter.

Topping:

4. In medium bowl with electric mixer, combine Bisquick, sugar and butter. Beat thoroughly.

5. Sprinkle topping, chocolate chips and nuts over top of cake.

6. Bake 55 minutes or until top of cake is golden brown.

DELICIOUS Declarations!

Too much of a good thing is wonderful.
♠ Mae West

Nuts just take up space where chocolate ought to be.
♠ Unknown

Save Earth. It's the only planet with chocolate.
♠ Anonymous

Nothing chocolate, nothing gained.
♠ Anonymous

Money talks. Chocolate sings. Beautifully.
♠ Unknown, *The Rules of Chocolate*

Chocolate: Here today…gone today!
♠ Bumper Sticker

Las cosas claras y el chocolate espeso. (Ideas should be clear and chocolate thick.)
♠ Spanish proverb

Life is like a box of chocolates—you never know what you're gonna get.
♠ Forrest Gump, *Forrest Gump*

There's more to life than chocolate, but not right now.
♠ Unknown

CHOCOLATE CHERRY BREAD

Difficulty: ♠ ♠
Preparation Time: 20 minutes
Yield: 8 servings

¾ cup sugar
1 cup milk
⅓ cup vegetable oil
2 large eggs
2½ cups flour
½ cup cocoa
1 teaspoon baking soda
½ teaspoon baking powder
1 cup maraschino cherries, drained
½ cup pecans or walnuts, chopped

1.   Heat oven to 350°. Grease 9x5x3-inch loaf pan.

2.   In large bowl with electric mixer, beat together sugar, milk, oil and eggs.

3.   In large bowl, mix remaining dry ingredients. Add mixture to milk batter. Stir in cherries and nuts. Pour batter into prepared loaf pan.

4.   Bake 55 minutes or until toothpick inserted into center comes out clean.

5.   Cool 10 minutes and remove from pan. Place on wire rack to continue cooling.

♠ Think of all the wonderful things you can do with chocolate. You can bake it, dip it, dust it, freeze it, pour it, shape it, sprinkle it, whip it and more. But most importantly…you can eat it!

1. The majority of the world's chocolate is made from which beans?
    a) Trinitario beans
    b) Criollo beans
    c) Forastero beans

2. Which is the only US state to grow cocoa beans used to produce chocolate?
    a) Alaska
    b) Texas
    c) California
    d) Hawaii

3. The world leader in cocoa bean production for chocolate is:
    a) Ivory Coast, Africa
    b) Brazil, South America
    c) Malaysia, Southeast Asia
    d) Nigeria, Africa

4. Which continent produces the most chocolate?
    a) South America
    b) North America
    c) Asia
    d) Africa

5. Which of the following chocolates contains the most chocolate liquor?
    a) Milk chocolate
    b) Dark chocolate
    c) White chocolate
    d) Bittersweet chocolate

♠ *Solutions on page 141*

CHOCOLATE COVERED STRAWBERRIES & BANANAS

Difficulty: ♠ ♠ ♠
Preparation Time: 55 minutes
Yield: 36 strawberries and 6 bananas

Strawberries:
1 cup semi-sweet chocolate chips
1 cup white chocolate chips
1 tablespoon vegetable oil
Fresh strawberries with stems, rinsed and patted dry (You may substitute fresh pineapple or kiwi fruit)

Bananas:
3 bananas
6 wooden ice cream sticks (wooden skewers or chopsticks also work)
1½ cups semi-sweet chocolate chips
1 tablespoon vegetable oil
½ cup unsalted roasted peanuts, chopped (optional)
¼ cup shredded coconut (optional)

Strawberries:

1. Line cookie sheet small enough to fit in your refrigerator with aluminum foil.

2. In double boiler over hot water, melt and stir white chocolate chips with ½ tablespoon of oil until smooth. Keep chocolate over heat.

3. Grasp stem of strawberry and dip two-thirds in warm chocolate. Use a knife to help smooth on chocolate, if needed.

4. Put dipped fruit on cookie sheet and place in refrigerator. Cool at least 15 minutes before serving.

5. Repeat this process for semi-sweet chocolate.

Bananas:

6. Peel each banana and cut in half widthwise. Insert wooden stick into cut end of each banana half. Place in large plastic bag and seal tightly. Freeze at least 3 hours.

7. Line cookie sheet small enough to fit in your freezer with aluminum foil.

8. Place peanuts and coconut in 9x1½-inch pie pan or other shallow dish.

9. In double boiler over hot water, melt and stir chocolate chips and oil until smooth. Keep chocolate over heat and remove bananas from freezer.

10. Dip banana into melted chocolate. Use a knife to help smooth on chocolate to ensure each banana is covered completely. Immediately roll in peanuts and coconut.

11. Place on cookie sheet and return to freezer at least 20 minutes before serving. To store, return bananas to plastic bag and seal.

12. To serve, remove from freezer and set out at room temperature 10 to 15 minutes before eating.

Impress your friends with tuxedo strawberries: These require a double dip. Carefully grasp stem of strawberry and dip front side in white chocolate. Place on cookie sheet and chill in refrigerator 10 minutes. Remove from refrigerator and dip each side and back of strawberry in semi-sweet chocolate. The dipped sides should form a "V" on the white chocolate. Place some of the semi-sweet chocolate in pastry bag with writing tip, and add two buttons and bow tie to white front. Return strawberries to cookie sheet and chill in refrigerator at least 15 minutes before serving. Impressive!

COCONUT CHOCOLATE CHIP COOKIES

Difficulty: ♠ ♠
Preparation Time: 20 minutes
Yield: 40 cookies

2 cups flaked coconut
2 cups flour
¾ teaspoon baking soda
⅛ teaspoon salt
1 cup butter or margarine, softened
1½ cups light brown sugar
¾ teaspoon almond extract
¼ teaspoon vanilla
2 cups semi-sweet chocolate chips

1. Heat oven to 350°. Lightly grease two cookie sheets.

2. Spread coconut on 1 cookie sheet and toast 10 minutes. Stir coconut every 2–3 minutes to prevent burning. When done, remove coconut from oven and cool completely.

3. In large bowl with electric mixer, beat butter and brown sugar on medium speed until light and fluffy. Add in eggs, almond extract and vanilla and beat well.

4. In medium bowl, combine flour, baking soda and salt. Add dry ingredients to egg batter. Fold in toasted coconut and chocolate chips.

5. Drop batter by heaping spoonfuls about 1½ to 2 inches apart on cookie sheets.

6. Bake 12–14 minutes or until golden brown.

7. Remove from oven and serve warm.

CHOCOLATE FIGS & DATES

Difficulty: ♠
Preparation Time: 10 minutes
Yield: 20 candies

½ cup semi-sweet chocolate chips, melted
20 large dried figs or dates
¼ cup miniature marshmallows
⅛ cup walnuts or pecans

1. With a knife, slice side of each fig or date and place 1–2 nuts or marshmallows inside each fruit.

2. Dip filled figs or dates halfway into melted chocolate.

3. Place on wax paper until chocolate hardens.

♠ Top Ten Excuses for Eating Chocolate:

1. I love it.
2. I love it.
3. I love it.
4. I love it.
5. I love it.
6. I love it.
7. I love it.
8. I love it.
9. I love it.
10. I love it.

(On the other hand, who needs an excuse?)

TANTALIZING Tidbits

♠ One ounce of milk chocolate contains about six milligrams of caffeine; about the same as the amount found in a cup of decaffeinated coffee.

♠ Cocoa flavanols may support healthy blood vessels and circulation, according to research presented at the National Academies in Washington, DC.

♠ Chocolate provides a number of nutrients the body requires daily. A milk chocolate bar weighing 1.4 ounces contains approximately 3 grams of protein, 15% of the daily value of riboflavin, 9% of the daily value of calcium, and 7% of the daily value of iron. Almonds and peanuts added to chocolate increase the nutrients in a bar. This is particularly true for protein.

♠ Chocolate is rich in carbohydrates and is an excellent source of quick energy. It also contains minute amounts of the stimulating alkaloids theobromine and caffeine, which activate the pleasure centers of the brain.

♠ According to a Harvard University study of 7,581 male students, those who consume a moderate amount of chocolate and candy live nearly one year longer than those who abstained.

♠ Dirk Taubert, MD, Ph.D. and colleagues shed light on the health benefits of dark chocolate in *The Journal of the American Medical Association*. According to their studies, "Dark chocolate—not white chocolate—lowers high blood pressure."

CHOCOLATE PEAR CAKE

Difficulty: ♠ ♠ ♠
Preparation Time: 20 minutes
Yield: 10 servings

1 cup flour
3 tablespoons unsweetened cocoa
½ teaspoon baking powder
3 large pears, peeled, cored and cut into ⅛'s lengthwise (an apple slicer works well for cutting)
⅔ cup granulated sugar
½ cup butter or margarine, softened
2 large eggs
½ cup semi-sweet chocolate chips
¼ teaspoon cinnamon
Powdered sugar

1. Heat oven to 350°. Grease and flour bottom and sides of 9-inch springform pan.

2. In small bowl, combine flour, cocoa and baking powder.

3. Place granulated sugar in large mixing bowl.

4. Remove 1 tablespoon of sugar and set aside in cup.

5. Add butter to sugar in bowl and beat with electric mixer on medium speed 2 minutes until light and fluffy. Beat in eggs one at a time until blended. On low speed, beat in dry ingredient mixture. Stir in chocolate chips.

6. Spread 1½ cups batter in prepared pan. On top of batter, arrange pear slices in circular pattern with tapered ends toward center, overlapping around edge of pan (do not cover center with fruit).

7. Combine cinnamon and reserved sugar. Sprinkle over pears.

8. Spread light coating of remaining batter on top of pears.

9. Bake 30 minutes or until a toothpick inserted in the center of cake comes out clean.

10. Cool cake in pan on wire rack.

11. Remove side of pan and sift powdered sugar over top. Serve warm or at room temperature.

CHOCOLATE PINEAPPLE SQUARES

Difficulty: ♠ ♠ ♠
Preparation Time: 25 minutes
Yield: 12 bars

¾ cup shortening
1½ cups sugar
1½ teaspoons vanilla
3 large eggs
1 cup flour
1 teaspoon baking powder
½ teaspoon salt
½ teaspoon cinnamon
¼ cup pecans or other nut, chopped
2 ounces unsweetened chocolate
1 cup pineapple, crushed and drained
Powdered sugar

1. Heat oven to 350º. Grease and flour bottom and sides of 9x9x2-inch pan.

2. In large bowl with electric mixer, cream shortening, sugar and vanilla. Beat in eggs.

3. In small bowl, combine dry ingredients. Stir into egg mixture.

4. Divide batter into 2 bowls.

5. Melt chocolate and stir in nuts. Add chocolate and nuts to one half of batter. Add pineapple to other half of batter.

6. Spread chocolate and nuts mixture evenly into pan. Carefully spread pineapple mixture over chocolate mixture.

7. Bake 35 minutes. Sprinkle with powdered sugar.

1. According to the slogan, "There's no wrong way to eat a _____?"
   a) Three Musketeers
   b) Reese's Peanut Butter Cup
   c) Big Hunk
   d) Tootsie Roll

2. Whose slogan used to be, "Don't let hunger happen to you!"
   a) Hershey's Chocolate Bar
   b) Twix
   c) Snickers
   d) 100 Grand

3. "It's all in the mix." The answer has got to be _____.
   a) Kit Kat
   b) M&M's
   c) Baby Ruth
   d) Twix

4. "Sometimes you feel like a nut, sometimes you don't." One of the candy bars is Mounds, and the other is _____.
   a) Snickers
   b) PayDay
   c) Look
   d) Almond Joy

5. Bart Simpson warns "Nobody better lay a finger on my _____."
   a) 100 Grand
   b) Snickers
   c) Butterfinger
   d) Baby Ruth

♠ *Solutions on page 142*

TOMATO SOUP CHOCOLATE CAKE

Difficulty: ♠ ♠
Preparation Time: 20 minutes
Yield: 12 servings

½ cup butter or margarine, softened
2 large eggs
1½ cups sugar
1 cup flour
1 cup whole wheat flour
½ cup cocoa
1 tablespoon baking powder
1 teaspoon baking soda
¼ cup water
10¾ ounces condensed tomato soup
1 cup pecans or other nut, chopped (optional)

1. Heat oven to 350°. Grease and flour bottom and sides of 13x9x2-inch pan.

2. In large bowl with electric mixer, cream together butter and sugar. Add eggs, and beat thoroughly.

3. In medium bowl, whisk together dry ingredients.

4. In small bowl, mix tomato soup and water.

5. Alternately add dry ingredients and soup mixture to creamed mixture. Fold in pecans. Pour into prepared pan.

6. Bake 35 minutes or until toothpick inserted into center comes out clean.

7. When cake has cooled, sprinkle with powdered sugar or frost with your favorite frosting.

♠ What do cannibals eat for lunch?
Answer: Chocolate covered aunts.

MILK

- Cheesecake
- Cheese Fudge
- Chocoholic Pie
- Fantasy Ice Cream
- Four-Layer Dessert*
- Hot Chocolate
- Milkshake
- Mousse Sundae
- Buttermilk Pound Cake
- Yogurt Crème

CHOCOLATE CHEESECAKE

Difficulty: ♠ ♠
Preparation Time: 20 minutes
Yield: 2 pies (12 servings)

2 chocolate graham cracker pie crusts
1 cup semi-sweet chocolate chips, melted
24 ounces cream cheese
1 cup sugar
2 large eggs
2 teaspoons cocoa
¼ teaspoon cinnamon
2 teaspoons vanilla
1½ cups sour cream

1. Heat oven to 350°.

2. In large bowl with electric mixer, beat cream cheese until smooth and creamy. Beat in sugar and eggs. Beat in melted chocolate, followed by cocoa, vanilla and sour cream. Pour half of batter into each pie crust.

3. Cool 1 hour.

4. Refrigerate at least 4 hours before serving.

♠ An elderly man was at home, dying in bed. He smelled the aroma of his favorite chocolate chip cookies baking. He wanted one last cookie before he died. He fell out of bed, crawled to the landing, rolled down the stairs, and crawled into the kitchen where his wife was busily baking cookies.

With waning strength he crawled to the table and was just barely able to lift his withered arm to the cookie sheet.

As he grasped a warm, moist, chocolate chip cookie, his wife whacked his hand with a spatula.

"Why did you do that?" he whispered.

"They're for the funeral," she answered.

DELICIOUS Declarations!

Put "eat chocolate" at the top of your list of things to do today. That way, at least you'll get one thing done.
♠ Unknown

The 12-step chocoholics program: Never be more than twelve steps away from chocolate!
♠ Terry Moore

Elementary school teachers stated by a 4:1 margin that they would prefer receiving a box of chocolates instead of the traditional shiny red apple, in a nationwide survey conducted by the National Confectioners Association. 62% of elementary school teachers said they eat chocolate at least once a week.
♠ 2000 Society for the Advancement of Teachers, *USA Today*

Strength is the capacity to break a chocolate bar into four pieces with your bare hands—and then eat just one of the pieces.
♠ Judith Viorst

Emergency Alert: If wearer of this shirt is found vacant, listless, or depressed, administer chocolate immediately.
♠ Saying on a t-shirt

Researchers have discovered that chocolate produced some of the same reactions in the brain as marijuana. The researchers also discovered other similarities between the two, but can't remember what they are.
♠ Matt Lauer, NBC's *Today Show*

CHEESE FUDGE

Difficulty: ♠
Preparation Time: 10 minutes
Yield: 16 pieces

½ cup butter or margarine
½ cup Velveeta® cheese
¼ cup cocoa
3½ cups powdered sugar
½ cup walnuts or other nut, chopped (optional)
¾ teaspoon vanilla

1. Grease bottom and sides of 8x8x2-inch pan.

2. In medium microwave-safe bowl, melt butter and cheese on high 45 seconds or until cheese melts. Remove from microwave and stir. Add in remaining ingredients and mix. Spread batter in pan.

3. Refrigerate and let set.

4. Cut into squares and serve. Store in refrigerator.

1. Which one of the following generally does not mix well with chocolate?
   a) Bourbon
   b) White Wine
   c) Fine Cognac
   d) Coffee
   e) Water

2. Which of the following types of chocolate is often called "bitter" or "luxury" chocolate?
   a) Couverture
   b) Dark chocolate
   c) Milk chocolate
   d) White chocolate

3. Tabliering means:
   a) Tempering by hand.
   b) Enrobing liquid centers.
   c) Refining and rolling.
   d) Agitating a mixture over time.

4. Theobroma Cacao is the scientific name for the cocoa tree. When translated from Greek it means:
   a) Brown tree from abroad
   b) Drink of the gods
   c) Warm dark fluid
   d) Fat free

♠ *Solutions on page 142*

CHOCOHOLIC PIE

Difficulty: ♠ ♠
Preparation time: 20 minutes
Yield: 6 servings

1 chocolate cookie pie crust
4 cups chocolate ice cream, softened
1 cup whipped topping
⅓ cup milk chocolate chips
⅓ cup white chocolate chips
8 ounces chocolate whipped topping

1. In large bowl with electric mixer, beat together ice cream and whipped topping.

2. In medium bowl, mix together milk chocolate and white chocolate chips. Reserve 2 tablespoons. Add chips to ice cream mixture and stir to blend. Pour mixture into the pie crust and freeze 10 minutes.

3. Remove pie from freezer and cover with chocolate whipped topping. Sprinkle reserved chocolate chips on top. Return pie to freezer.

4. Before serving, set out at room temperature 20 minutes.

Another fun option: In pie crust, add bottom layer of 1½ cups chocolate ice cream and spread evenly. Add 1½ cups strawberry ice cream for middle layer. Add 1½ cups mint ice cream for top layer. Freeze and serve.

TANTALIZING
Tidbits

♠ To improve her memory, First Lady Eleanor Roosevelt ate three chocolate-covered garlic balls every morning.

♠ Henri Nestle was originally a baby food manufacturer. His research of condensed milk aided Swiss chocolatier Daniel Peter in successfully combining chocolate and milk to create a solid form. The result came in 1875 with the creation of milk chocolate. Peter worked diligently for eight years to invent the delicious treat.

♠ Christopher Columbus was the first European to taste chocolate. He came across the chance in 1502 on his fourth voyage to the New World.

♠ Casanova, fond of chocolate's divine properties, considered it an elixir of love.

♠ Queen Victoria was such a chocolate devotee that she sent 500,000 pounds of chocolate to her troops one Christmas.

♠ Albert Einstein approved the patent for the mold used to make the Toblerone chocolate bar during his tenure in Switzerland's patent office. Definitely a genius!

♠ Montezuma, the last Aztec ruler, personally consumed some fifty pitchers of chocolate drink each day and had two thousand pitchers prepared for members of his household.

♠ In 1861, Richard Cadbury invented the heart-shaped Valentine's Day chocolate box.

FANTASY ICE CREAM

Difficulty: ♠
Preparation Time: 10 minutes
Yield: 6 servings

1 cup chocolate sandwich cookies, crumbled
1 cup your favorite chocolate candy, chopped
1 quart vanilla ice cream, softened
4 ounces whipping cream

1. In medium bowl or blender, combine ice cream and whipping cream. Add crumbled cookies and chopped candies and stir until blended.

2. Cover and freeze at least 30 minutes before serving.

♠ Top 10 Reasons Why Chocolate is Better Than a Vacation:

1. You can afford chocolate.
2. You do not need a reservation.
3. Weather does not matter.
4. You do not need to schedule chocolate.
5. You do not have to board your pets.
6. No packing.
7. Chocolate always speaks your language.
8. No sunburn.
9. You will not lose your traveler's checks while eating chocolate.
10. No postcards to send.

FOUR-LAYER CHOCOLATE CHIP DESSERT

Difficulty: ♠ ♠
Preparation Time: 30 minutes
Yield: 12 servings

1 cup flour
1 cup walnuts, finely chopped
½ cup butter or margarine, softened
8 ounces cream cheese
1 cup powdered sugar
12 ounces whipping cream
⅛ cup milk chocolate chips
3–4 ounces vanilla instant pudding
3–4 ounces chocolate instant pudding
3 cups low-fat milk

1. Heat oven to 350º. Grease bottom and sides of 13x9x2-inch pan.

2. In medium bowl, mix together flour, walnuts and butter. Press mixture into pan.

3. Bake 25 minutes.

4. Remove from oven and let cool 15 minutes.

5. In medium bowl with electric mixer, beat cream cheese, powdered sugar and 4 ounces whipping cream. Spread mixture over cool crust. Sprinkle top with half of chocolate chips.

6. Mix together vanilla pudding, chocolate pudding and milk. Beat until stiff, then pour over previous layer.

7. Spread remaining 8 ounces of whipping cream over top layer.

8. Sprinkle top with remaining chocolate chips and walnuts.

9. Refrigerate at least 1 hour before serving.

CHOCOLATE Challenge

1. In her book *Why Women Need Chocolate*, Debra Waterhouse shared the results of her survey that showed:
   a) 50% of women would choose chocolate over sex.
   b) 68% of women reported cravings for chocolate.
   c) 22% more women than men were likely to choose chocolate to enhance their mood.
   d) All of the above

2. According to World Records™, the largest individual chocolate was made by Nestlé. How much did it weigh?
   a) 2,387 pounds
   b) 5,980 pounds
   c) 10,011 pounds
   d) 13,183 pounds

3. For which occasion is the most chocolate purchased?
   a) Halloween
   b) Christmas
   c) Valentine's Day
   d) Easter

4. The first North American chocolate factory was built by Dr. James Baker and John Hannon in:
   a) 1679
   b) 1765
   c) 1840
   d) 1901

5. In 1657 the first chocolate shop opened in:
   a) Vienna
   b) London
   c) Amsterdam
   d) Los Angeles

♠ *Solutions on page 142*

HOT WHITE CHOCOLATE

Difficulty: ♠
Preparation Time: 15 minutes
Yield: 8, eight-ounce cups

6 cups half-and-half
1¼ cups white chocolate chips
1 teaspoon ground cinnamon
¼ teaspoon ground nutmeg
½ teaspoon almond extract
1 tablespoon vanilla

1. In 4-quart saucepan, combine 1 cup half-and-half, chocolate chips, cinnamon and nutmeg. Stir continuously over low heat until chocolate chips are melted. Add remaining half-and-half. Cook and stir until mixture thoroughly heated. Remove from heat. Stir in almond extract and vanilla.

2. Serve immediately in coffee mugs. You may wish to top with whipping cream.

♠ Top 10 Reasons Why Chocolate is Better Than Air:

1. If you do not get any chocolate in three minutes, you will still be alive.
2. Chocolate smells better.
3. Chocolate has taste.
4. You can see chocolate.
5. You can embrace chocolate.
6. Chocolate will not mess up your hairdo.
7. Chocolate will not lift your skirt up.
8. Swallowing chocolate will not make you belch.
9. Big city chocolate is not polluted.
10. It is okay to be full of hot chocolate.

♠ According to many studies, chocolate is the number one food craved by women, but scientists are undecided as to why.

♠ Drinking chocolate mixed with milk, wine, or beer was considered a "must" at fashionable social events in the 17th century.

♠ *Palet* is the name for a thin, round wafer of chocolate. *Pavé* is the name for a square chocolate with rounded corners.

♠ Prince Albert orchestrated The Exposition in London in 1851. It was there that citizens of the United States were first introduced to bonbons, chocolate creams, hard candies (called "boiled sweets") and caramels.

♠ Children are more likely to drink chocolate milk than plain milk. Studies have shown that the amount of chocolate milk left undrunk by children in grades 1 through 5 was about two-thirds less than when plain milk was served.

♠ Per a national survey, 80% of US teachers in grades kindergarten through 8th grade have received chocolate as a gift from their students.

♠ How do you spell chocolate?
Chocolat in French
Cioccolato in Italian
Czekolada in Polish
Chocolate in Spanish
Schokolade in German
Sjokolade in Norwegian
Choklad in Swedish

MILKSHAKE

Difficulty: ♠
Preparation Time: 5 minutes
Yield: 2 servings

1 cup low-fat milk
½ banana
2 teaspoons peanut butter
2 cups chocolate ice cream
1 tablespoon maple syrup
Whipped cream (optional)

1. Place all ingredients, except whipped cream, in blender. Mix until blended and smooth.

2. Pour half mixture into each glass and garnish with whipped cream. Serve immediately.

Create your own delicious milkshake combinations: Test different flavors of ice cream or frozen yogurt. Try using fruits, cookies and various chocolate candies. Blend thoroughly before drinking.

♠ Chocolate bars are better than gold bars.

♠ Promise me anything, but give me chocolate.

CHOCOLATE MOUSSE SUNDAE

Difficulty: ♠
Preparation Time: 9 minutes
Yield: 8 servings

5–6 ounces chocolate instant pudding
3 cups low-fat milk
8 ounces whipped topping
½ cup miniature milk chocolate chips

1. In large bowl with electric mixer, combine instant pudding mix and milk. Fold in whipped cream. Spoon into 8 6-ounce ramekins.

2. Refrigerate 1 hour. Serve.

Optional:
3. Top with whipping cream, grated chocolate and a cherry.

THE NICE THING
ABOUT STANDARDS
IS THAT THERE
ARE SO MANY TO
CHOOSE FROM.
I CHOOSE THE
CHOCOLATE
STANDARD.

CHOCOLATE BUTTERMILK POUND CAKE

Difficulty: ♠♠
Preparation Time: 20 minutes
Yield: 10 servings

2 ounces unsweetened chocolate
1 teaspoon vegetable oil
½ cup margarine
2 cups sugar
2 large eggs
½ cup buttermilk
2 cups sifted flour
1 cup boiling water
1 teaspoon baking soda
1 tablespoon vanilla

1. In double boiler, melt chocolate and oil. Heat oven to 325°. Grease and flour 12-cup bundt cake pan.

2. In large bowl, cream together margarine and 2 cups sugar. Add eggs and buttermilk to margarine mixture. Stir in 2 cups flour.

3. Boil 1 cup water and pour ½ cup water into warm chocolate and oil.

4. Add baking soda to remaining ½ cup water. Blend into chocolate mixture while still over heat. Stir well.

5. Slowly add chocolate mixture and vanilla to batter, mixing thoroughly. Pour into bundt pan.

6. Bake 1 hour and 15 minutes.

7. Dust cake with powdered sugar.

♠ What did the dairy farmer do at the chocolate factory?
Answer: Milk chocolates.

DELICIOUS Declarations!

Chocolate doesn't make the world go 'round, but it certainly makes the ride worthwhile.
♠ Unknown

Chocolate causes certain endocrine glands to secrete hormones that affect your feelings and behavior by making you happy. Therefore, it counteracts depression, in turn reducing the stress of depression. Your stress-free life helps you maintain a youthful disposition, both physically and mentally. So, eat lots of chocolate!
♠ Elaine Sherman, *Book of Divine Indulgences*

My love affair with chocolate makes me want to celebrate every day.
♠ Marcel Desaulniers, *Celebrate with Chocolate*

"I drink chocolate, it makes me happy, my heart rejoice."
♠ Song of the ancient Aztecs

Chocolate is nature's way of making up for Mondays.
♠ Anonymous

If I have chocolate around I will eat it. I love it, I love it, I love it. I like a piece every day.
♠ Julia Louis-Dreyfus

Chocolate is cheaper than therapy and you don't need an appointment.
♠ Anonymous

CHOCOLATE STRAWBERRY YOGURT CRÈME

Difficulty: ♠ ♠
Preparation Time: 20 minutes
Yield: 8 servings

1 cup sugar
⅓ cup cocoa
1 envelope unflavored gelatin
1⅓ cups low-fat milk
2 cups nonfat vanilla yogurt
1½ teaspoons vanilla
8 fresh strawberries, sliced
Mint leaves (optional)

1. In 3-quart saucepan, mix together sugar, cocoa and gelatin. Stir in milk and let stand 5 minutes. Cook over medium-high heat, stirring constantly, until mixture comes to a boil and gelatin is dissolved. Remove from heat and cool 8 minutes.

2. Add yogurt and vanilla to mixture and blend until well combined. Pour into 8 6-ounce ramekins.

3. Refrigerate and let set at least 4 hours.

4. Add 1 sliced strawberry and mint leaves to top of each cup and serve.

MEATS, BEANS & NUTS

- ▲ Almond Macaroons
- ▲ Barbeque Sauce
- ▲ Chili
- ▲ Chocochiladas
- ▲ Ole Mole Chicken
- ▲ Pecan Tarts
- ▲ Spicy Lentil & Vegetable Soup
- ▲ Tenderloin Con Queso*
- ▲ Tropical Mole Over Grilled Swordfish
- ▲ White Chocolate Pecan Bark

WHITE CHOCOLATE ALMOND MACAROONS

Difficulty: ♠ ♠
Preparation Time: 15 minutes
Yield: 32 cookies

7 large egg whites
½ teaspoon salt
1 cup granulated sugar
½ teaspoon almond extract
1 teaspoon vanilla
1⅔ cups flour, sifted
2 tablespoons butter or margarine
4 cups coconut flakes
½ cup almonds, chopped
⅓ cup white chocolate chips
½ cup semi-sweet chocolate chips (optional)

1. Heat oven to 325°. Lightly grease and flour 2 cookie sheets.

2. In large bowl with electric mixer, combine eggs, sugar and salt. Beat 8 minutes.

3. Beat in vanilla and almond extract. Fold in flour and mix well. Add coconut and almonds.

4. In small microwave-safe bowl, heat butter on high until melted. Cool.

5. In small microwave-safe bowl, melt white chocolate on high 75 seconds. Stir chocolate until smooth and add melted butter. Mix well.

6. Add chocolate and butter to coconut mixture and stir until thoroughly combined. Add semi-sweet chocolate chips and mix well.

7. Drop batter by heaping teaspoonful onto prepared cookie sheets, about two inches apart.

8. Bake 18 minutes or until cookies are crusty and lightly browned.

9. Remove from oven and serve warm.

CHOCOLATE BARBEQUE SAUCE

Difficulty: ♠ ♠
Preparation Time: 30 minutes
Yield: 12 servings

1 cup chopped onion
¼ cup butter or margarine
2 tablespoons chili powder
1 teaspoon oregano
2 tablespoons marjoram
1½ teaspoons rosemary
5 cloves garlic, chopped
1 teaspoon garlic salt
1 ounce baking chocolate, grated
2 cups water
4 tablespoons cider vinegar
16 ounces tomato paste
4 tablespoons light brown sugar

1. In 8-inch skillet, sauté onion in butter over medium heat 3 minutes. Add chili powder, oregano, marjoram, rosemary, garlic, and garlic salt. Cover and simmer 10 minutes, stirring occasionally. Add chocolate and stir constantly until melted.

2. Place remaining four ingredients in blender or food processor. Add onion mixture and blend 3 minutes.

3. Use when basting your favorite grilled meats and poultry.

♠ In a restaurant:
Customer: "What flavors of milkshakes do you sell?"
Waiter, whispering: "Chocolate, vanilla and strawberry."
Customer: "Can you speak up? Do you have laryngitis?"
Waiter: "No. Just chocolate, vanilla and strawberry."

1. Hot Chocolate was a British group that played funk and disco music. Which song was their last Top 40 hit?
   a) *Emma*
   b) *Disco Queen*
   c) *You Sexy Thing*
   d) *Every 1's a Winner*

2. Which of the following chocolate movies was first to debut?
   a) *Bread and Chocolate*
   b) *Like Water for Chocolate*
   c) *Chocolat*
   d) *Willy Wonka and the Chocolate Factory*

3. Which of the following is the title of a published book?
   a) *The Chocolate Frog Frame-Up: A Chocoholic Mystery*
   b) *Max's Chocolate Chicken*
   c) *The Chocolate Cow*
   d) *The Chocolate Dinosaurs*
   e) All of the above

4. Which of the following bands changed their name to "Captain" and then to "Zero Tolerance"?
   a) My Friend the Chocolate Cake
   b) Chocolate Frosted Sugar Bombz
   c) Chocolate Weasel
   d) White Chocolate

♠ *Solutions on page 142*

CHOCOLATE CHILI

When living in the greater Cincinnati area, this type of chili was often served over spaghetti and topped with grated cheddar and diced onions.

Difficulty: ♠ ♠ ♠ ♠
Preparation Time: 2 hours
Yield: 4–6 servings

2 pounds lean ground beef, pork or poultry
3 tablespoons cooking oil or butter
2 onions, chopped
3 cups water
2 cups tomato juice
¾ cup canned diced tomatoes with chilies
2 tablespoons hot sauce
1 clove garlic, crushed
4 tablespoons chili powder
3 tablespoons oregano
3 tablespoons ground cumin
3 tablespoons cocoa
2 tablespoons cinnamon
2 tablespoons garlic salt
2 teaspoons black pepper
4 tablespoons cornmeal
2½ cups pinto or kidney beans, drained

1. In 4-quart Dutch oven, heat oil over medium heat. Add meat and onions and sauté 15 minutes. Add water, tomato juice, diced tomatoes, hot sauce, garlic, chili powder, oregano, cumin, cocoa, cinnamon, garlic, and pepper. Mix well. Boil 5 minutes. Reduce heat to medium-low and simmer uncovered 1 hour, stirring often.

2. Stir in cornmeal and beans and simmer 10 minutes or until thick.

3. Season to taste and serve.

TANTALIZING Tidbits

♠ A perfected steam engine, which mechanized the cocoa grinding process, sped the transition from hand manufacture to mass production. By 1730, chocolate had dropped in price from $3 or more per pound to a price affordable by all.

♠ The first machine-made chocolate was produced in 1780 in Barcelona, Spain.

♠ The Ivory Coast, Ghana, and Indonesia account for 70% of the world's cocoa production.

♠ Swiss chocolate makers are legally bound to use their country's own raw materials, many of which are price-controlled.

♠ Chocolate is made with cocoa butter, derived from cocoa beans. Cocoa butter has a melting point of 97°F. Over time, the cost of cocoa butter has risen, so chocolate manufacturers have begun to use cocoa butter alternatives such as coconut oil and palm oil. These butters have a much higher melting point and require a process called "hydrogenation" to alter them. Hydrogenation involves inserting hydrogen gas into hot oil at very high temperatures. The result is altered butters with lower solidifying and melting points, similar to that of cocoa butter. It is hydrogen that is the secret behind your chocolate's melt-in-your mouth properties.

♠ The first US Standards of Identity for Chocolate and Cocoa products were established by the US Food and Drug Administration on December 6, 1944. The Standards of Identity for Chocolate and Cacoa products ensure that criteria for high quality products and consumer trust are maintained. The standards were updated in the 1990s. There is now an effort being made to create common US and European chocolate standards.

CHOCOCHILADAS

Difficulty: ♦♦♦♦♦
Preparation Time: 60 minutes
Yield: 8–10 servings

1 pound ground meat (beef, pork or poultry)
1 onion, diced
¼ cup butter or cooking oil
3 teaspoons chili powder
1½ teaspoons paprika
2 teaspoons garlic salt
2 teaspoons black pepper
½ ounce unsweetened chocolate, grated
1 teaspoon cinnamon
1 teaspoon ground cloves
¾ cup canned diced tomatoes with chilies
24 ounces canned tomato sauce
2½ cups water
4 cups cheddar cheese, shredded
12 flour tortillas

1. In 4-quart saucepan or 4-quart Dutch oven, sauté meat and onion in butter 10 minutes. Drain off excess fat.

2. Add chili powder, paprika, garlic salt, pepper, grated chocolate, cinnamon, ground cloves, tomatoes, tomato sauce, and water. Bring to boil.

3. Reduce heat to medium-low and simmer uncovered 35 minutes or until sauce is thick.

4. Heat oven to 350°. Set out 15x10 baking dish.

5. Assemble each enchilada as follows: Dip tortilla into sauce mixture to soften and place on plate. Using a slotted spoon, spread 1 heaping tablespoon of meat and onion from sauce mixture into center of tortilla. Top with 1 heaping tablespoon of cheese. Roll and place seam side down in baking dish.

6. Pour remaining sauce over enchiladas and top with remaining cheese.

7. Bake 15 minutes until cheese is melted.

OLE MOLE CHICKEN

Difficulty: ♠ ♠ ♠
Preparation Time: 30 minutes
Yield: 6 servings

6 boneless, skinless chicken breasts
Garlic salt
Black pepper
3 tablespoons melted butter or cooking oil

Mole Sauce:
15 ounces diced tomatoes with chilies, undrained
¾ cup salsa
4 teaspoons unsweetened cocoa
1 teaspoon cumin
1 teaspoon oregano
2 tablespoons chili powder
2 teaspoons peanut butter
3 cloves garlic, diced
Dash of cloves
Dash of nutmeg
Dash of allspice
2 tablespoons sesame seeds

1. Heat oven to 350º.

2. Place chicken in 11x7x1½-inch baking dish. Salt and pepper to taste and drizzle with butter or oil.

3. Bake 40 minutes or until cooked through.

Mole sauce:

4. Mix all ingredients in 4-quart saucepan and bring to boil.

5. Reduce heat and simmer 15 minutes, stirring occasionally.

6. Serve warm over chicken breasts.

♠ *Do Not Disturb:* Chocolate fantasy in progress.

DELICIOUS Declarations!

I don't understand why so many "so-called" chocolate lovers complain about the calories in chocolate, when all true chocoholics know that it is a vegetable. It comes from the cocoa bean and beans are veggies— 'nuff said.
♠ Unknown

Exercise is a dirty word. Every time I hear it, I wash my mouth out with chocolate.
♠ Unknown

Chemically speaking, chocolate really is the world's perfect food.
♠ Michael Levine, nutrition researcher as quoted in *The Emperors of Chocolate: Inside the Secret World of Hershey and Mars*

If calories are an issue, store your chocolate on top of the refrigerator. Calories are afraid of heights, and they will jump out of the chocolate to protect themselves.
♠ Unknown, *The Rules of Chocolate*

There are four basic food groups: milk chocolate, dark chocolate, white chocolate, and chocolate truffles.
♠ Anonymous

Inside some of us is a thin person struggling to get out, but he/she can usually be sedated with a few pieces of chocolate.
♠ *Milpitas Mom's Favorite Jokes*

I have this theory that chocolate slows down the aging process. It may not be true, but do I dare take the chance?
♠ Unknown

PECAN TARTS

Difficulty: ♠ ♠
Preparation Time: 25 minutes
Yield: 18 tarts

6 ounces cream cheese, softened
1 cup butter or margarine, softened
2 cups flour, sifted

Filling:
3 large eggs
2 tablespoons butter or margarine, softened
2 teaspoons vanilla
¼ teaspoon salt
¾ cup pecans, chopped

1. Heat oven to 350°. Lightly grease and flour 2 12-cup muffin tins.

2. In medium bowl with electric mixer, combine cream cheese, butter and flour.

3. Form dough into balls roughly the size of a ping pong ball and press into muffin pan cups. Dough needs to cover bottom and two-thirds of sides of each cup. Set aside.

Filling:

4. In small bowl, beat eggs with fork.

5. In medium bowl with electric mixer, beat together eggs, 2 tablespoons butter, brown sugar, vanilla and salt.

6. Pour filling into crusts and fill until halfway full. Add pecan on top.

7. Bake 18–20 minutes.

8. Cool before removing from pan and serving.

_____ 1. Antonio Nunez Montoya, nicknamed "El Chocolate," was a famous gymnast.

_____ 2. Casanova claimed he drank chocolate instead of champagne.

_____ 3. Napoleon carried chocolate with him on his military campaigns.

_____ 4. Explorer Hernando Cortez discovered the Aztec Indians used cocoa beans to prepare a royal drink called "chocolatl."

_____ 5. The Hershey Chocolate Company was founded as a sideline by Milton Hershey whose caramel business was booming.

_____ 6. Godiva was founded over seventy-five years ago.

♠ *Solutions on page 143*

SPICY LENTIL & VEGETABLE SOUP

Difficulty: ♠ ♠
Preparation Time: 35 minutes
Yield: 4 servings

2 tablespoons olive oil
2 cloves garlic, minced
1 red onion, chopped
1 medium yellow squash, chopped
2 tomatillos, peeled and chopped
4 ounces canned diced jalapeños
18 ounces canned Lentil soup
14 ounces canned vegetable broth
11 ounces canned tomato soup
½ teaspoon coriander
1 teaspoon ground cumin
1 teaspoon dry cilantro
1 heaping tablespoon cocoa
Salt and pepper to taste

1.   In 3-quart saucepan, heat oil on medium. Add garlic, onion, squash, tomatillos and jalapeños.

2.   Cook 10 minutes, stirring frequently.

3.   Mix 3 soups, seasonings and cocoa. Bring to boil.

4.   Reduce heat and simmer 10 minutes.

Note: If you prefer a milder taste, reduce jalapeños and/or cumin.

CHOCOLATE TENDERLOIN CON QUESO

Difficulty: ♠ ♠ ♠
Preparation Time: 30 minutes
Yield: 6 servings

6 serving size pieces of beef tenderloin (approximately 2 pounds)
Garlic salt
Black pepper
1 teaspoon chili powder
¼ cup butter or margarine
1 cup onion, diced
2 cloves garlic, crushed
½ cup white wine
½ cup water
1 ounce baking chocolate, grated
12 ounces Queso Fresco, crumbled (or grated mozzarella cheese)
3 tablespoons dry cilantro

1. Season steaks to taste with salt, pepper and chili powder.

2. In 12-inch skillet or 4-quart Dutch oven, melt butter over medium heat and cook steaks until browned on both sides. Add butter, onion, garlic and white wine and stir. Cover and simmer 15 minutes.

3. Add chocolate and simmer 10 minutes.

4. Slice steaks in half and place in single layer in 13x9x2-inch pan. Pour sauce evenly over meat.

5. Top meat with cheese and cilantro.

6. Broil 4 minutes or until cheese is melted.

♠ An ice cream salesman was found dead in his van covered in chocolate sauce and nuts. Police suspect that he may have topped himself.

MEET MY DOG HERSHEY, MY CAT CADBURY
AND MY BIRDS COUVERTURE AND COCOA.

TANTALIZING Tidbits

♠ See's Candies was founded in 1921. They make over 100 varieties of candies, maintaining strict adherence to their motto, "Quality Without Compromise."

♠ The OREO Chocolate Sandwich Cookie first appeared in 1912.

♠ In 2000, after forty-six years as "Plain M&M's," Mars changed the candy's name to "Milk Chocolate M&M's."

♠ General Mills Cocoa Puffs and Kellogg's Cocoa Krispies were both introduced in 1958.

♠ In was in Youngstown, Ohio in 1920 that Harry Burt invented the chocolate-covered vanilla ice cream bar on a stick. Good Humor Ice Cream was born shortly thereafter.

♠ Meantime Brewing in South London launched Chocolate Beer in February 2004.

♠ In the 1930s, ads for Ovaltine extolled the virtues of the drink and "how it quickly brings sound sleep."

♠ Several companies now offer personalized chocolates that have a layer of delicious milk chocolate topped with your custom design printed in edible ink.

♠ The tasty chocolaty beverage from Masterfoods called CocoaVia™ contains more than 100 milligrams of natural antioxidants, just 69 calories, and only 0.6 grams fat per 85 milliliter bottle.

♠ Bosco Chocolate Syrup was first made in 1928.

TROPICAL MOLE OVER GRILLED SWORDFISH

Difficulty: ▲ ▲ ▲ ▲ ▲
Preparation Time: 90 minutes
Yield: 6 servings

3 tablespoons olive oil or butter
1 red onion, chopped
4 cloves garlic, chopped
⅓ cup sesame seeds
3 cups clam stock
2 medium yellow peppers, chopped
1 mango, peeled and chopped
2 tomatillos, peeled and chopped
3 tablespoons golden raisins
1 ounce white chocolate, chopped
1 tablespoon honey
1 teaspoon ground cloves
Salt and pepper to taste
2 cups tortilla chips, broken up
6 swordfish steaks
3 tablespoons olive oil
Garlic salt and lemon pepper to taste

1. In 4-quart saucepan or 12-inch skillet, heat oil or butter and sauté onion and garlic 5 minutes. Add sesame seeds, clam stock, yellow peppers, mango, tomatillos, and golden raisins.

2. Cook uncovered over medium-high heat 30 minutes.

3. In food processor or blender, blend chips and onion mixture until smooth.

4. Pour mixture into clean 4-quart saucepan and cook over medium heat 25 minutes, stirring occasionally. Add chocolate, honey, cloves, salt and pepper and cook 5 minutes, stirring constantly.

Fish:

5. Brush fish steaks with oil and season both sides with garlic salt and lemon pepper.

6. Grill steaks over medium heat until they flake easily with a fork.

7. Serve fish immediately with warm mole sauce.

WHITE CHOCOLATE PECAN BARK

Difficulty: ♠
Preparation Time: 15 minutes
Yield: 1.25 pounds

2 cups white chocolate chips
1 tablespoon butter or margarine
1 tablespoon vegetable oil
½ teaspoon vanilla (optional)
1 cup pecans or other nut, coarsely chopped

1. Line cookie sheet with wax paper.

2. In double boiler, combine chocolate, butter and oil. Stir constantly until chocolate is melted and smooth. Remove melted chocolate from heat and stir in nuts.

3. Spoon chocolate mixture onto prepared cookie sheet and spread as desired.

4. Refrigerate 30 minutes or until set.

5. Separate chocolate sheet from wax paper. Break into pieces. Store in covered container in refrigerator.

A fun alternative to this recipe is to make marbled bark: Replace 1 cup white chocolate chips with 1 cup semi-sweet chocolate chips. Melt white chocolate and semi-sweet chocolate separately. Stir half of nuts into each mixture. Alternately spoon white chocolate and semi-sweet chocolate mixtures onto prepared cookie sheet. Swirl top with a butter knife. Refrigerate until set.

♠ While swimming in the ocean, a guy found a bottle. He opened it and out popped a genie who gave him three wishes. The guy wished for a million dollars, and POOF! there was a million dollars. Then he wished for a convertible, and POOF! there was a convertible. And then he wished he could be irresistible to all women and POOF!…he turned into a box of chocolates.

FATS & SWEETS

- ▲ Biscuits
- ▲ Chocolate Chip Cookies
- ▲ Coconut Cake
- ▲ Crispy Cinnamon Strips
- ▲ Marshmallow Pie
- ▲ Mousse
- ▲ Peppermint Patty Brownies
- ▲ Raspberry Terrine*
- ▲ Toffee
- ▲ Turtle Bars

CHOCOLATE CREAM BISCUITS

Difficulty: ♠ ♠ ♠
Preparation Time: 20 minutes
Yield: 12 biscuits

1 cup flour
¼ teaspoon ground nutmeg
¼ teaspoon salt
1 tablespoon sugar
¾ cup water
6 tablespoons unsalted butter
3 large eggs
3 cups vanilla ice cream

Sauce:
10 ounces unsweetened or semi-sweet chocolate
½ cup water

1. Heat oven to 400°. Grease cookie sheet.

2. In small bowl, combine flour, nutmeg, salt and sugar.

3. In 3-quart saucepan bring ¾ cup water and butter to boil. Reduce heat to low and add flour mixture. Cook 3 minutes, stirring constantly. Remove from heat.

4. In small bowl, beat eggs with fork and add to mixture. Beat well.

5. Set heaping tablespoons of dough in 12 round mounds on cookie sheet.

6. Bake 28–30 minutes or until biscuits are golden brown.

7. Turn oven temperature down to 200° and cut small slit in side of each biscuit.

8. Bake 10 minutes with oven door slightly open. When done, remove biscuits from oven and cool.

Sauce:

9. In double-boiler, melt and combine chocolate with ½ cup water. Stir until chocolate mixture is smooth.

10. Slice biscuits in half, add vanilla ice cream between halves and pour chocolate sauce over biscuits. Serve immediately.

DELICIOUS Declarations!

There's nothing better than a good friend, except a good friend with chocolate.
♠ Linda Grayson, *The Pickwick Papers*

Sisters share laughter, tears and lots of chocolate.
♠ Unknown

After about twenty years of marriage, I'm finally starting to scratch the surface of [what women want.] And I think the answer lies somewhere between conversation and chocolate.
♠ Mel Gibson as quoted in *US Magazine*

There's nothing that the taste of chocolate—and the Lord—can't fix.
♠ Peggy Bohanon, *peggiesplace.com*

Friends are the chocolate chips in the cookies of life.
♠ Anonymous

Giving chocolate to others is an intimate form of communication; a sharing of deep, dark secrets.
♠ Milton Zelman, publisher of *Chocolate News*

Chocolate is the greatest gift to women ever created, next to the likes of Paul Newman and Gene Kelly. It's something that should be had on a daily basis.
♠ Sandra Bullock

Man cannot live by chocolate alone, but woman sure can.
♠ Anonymous

CHOCOLATE CHIP COOKIES

Difficulty: ♠♠
Preparation Time: 15 minutes
Yield: 24 cookies

⅓ cup shortening
⅓ cup butter
½ cup sugar
½ cup brown sugar
1 large egg
1 teaspoon vanilla
1½ cups flour
½ teaspoon baking soda
½ teaspoon salt
½ cup pecans or other nut, chopped (optional)
¾ cup milk chocolate chips
¾ cup white chocolate chips

1. Heat oven to 375°. Grease two cookie sheets.

2. In large bowl with electric mixer, cream shortening, butter and two sugars. Beat egg and vanilla into mixture. Combine remaining ingredients and mix well.

3. Drop batter onto cookie sheet in heaping teaspoons two inches apart.

4. Bake 10 minutes.

5. Remove from oven and serve warm.

♠ To make chocolate curls, find a nice chunk of room temperature chocolate. Draw a vegetable peeler along the smooth edge of the chocolate. Pick up the curls with a toothpick to keep them from breaking. For grated chocolate, use a chunk of cool, firm chocolate and a hand grater. Clean grater often with dry towel.

TANTALIZING
Tidbits

♠ The American Heart Association recommends a daily cholesterol intake that does not exceed 300 milligrams. A 1.65 ounce milk chocolate bar contains only 12 milligrams of cholesterol, while a 1 ounce piece of cheddar cheese contains 30 milligrams of cholesterol. Compared to cheddar cheese, chocolate is a low cholesterol food.

♠ Over the past two decades, research at the University of Pennsylvania and the US Naval Academy found that consumption of chocolate—even frequent daily dietary intake—had no effect on the incidence of acne.

♠ According to the book *Mood Foods* by William Vayda, the amino acid phenylthylamine found in chocolate acts as a painkiller and antidepressant, making chocolate the true "feel good food."

♠ 10% of the US Recommended Daily Allowance of iron is found in one ounce of baking chocolate or cocoa.

♠ The *Daily News Archive* says chocolate contains tannins, which are compounds that help prevent cavity-causing bacteria from sticking to the teeth and gums. An Academy of General Dentistry spokesman says studies have shown that eating chocolate has suppressed cavity development.

♠ Chocolate has long been heralded for its value as an energy source. A single chocolate chip provides sufficient food energy for an adult to walk 150 feet. It would take only thirty-five chocolate chips to walk one mile, or 875,000 chips for an around-the-world hike.

WHITE CHOCOLATE COCONUT CAKE

Difficulty: ♠ ♠ ♠
Preparation Time: 45 minutes
Yield: 1 two-layer cake

½ cup water
½ cup white chocolate
1 cup butter
1 cup sugar
4 eggs, separated
2 teaspoons vanilla
2½ cups flour
1 teaspoon baking soda
1 teaspoon salt
1 cup plain yogurt
1 cup coconut flakes
½ cup pecans or walnuts, chopped

Frosting:
4 cups powdered sugar
½ teaspoon salt
5 tablespoons milk
6 tablespoons shortening
1½ teaspoons vanilla
1 cup coconut flakes

1. Heat oven to 350º. Grease and flour 2 9x9x2-inch pans.

2. In small microwave-safe bowl, heat water on high until boiling.

3. Add white chocolate to boiling water until melted. Cool.

4. In medium bowl, cream butter and sugar. Mix in egg yolks, chocolate mixture and vanilla.

5. In large bowl, combine flour, soda and salt.

6. Alternately add cream mixture and yogurt to dry mixture. Mix well.

7. In small bowl, stiffly beat egg whites.

8. Add whites and remaining ingredients to batter. Mix well.

9. Pour half of batter into each pan and bake 30 minutes.

Frosting:

10. In large bowl with electric mixer, combine sugar, salt, milk, shortening and vanilla. Beat at high speed until smooth.

11. Add coconut and beat 30 seconds.

12. Frost cake when cool.

♠ Top 10 Reasons Why Chocolate is Better Than a Car:

1. It is edible.
2. No payments.
3. Chocolate will not backfire.
4. Cops will not pull you over for eating chocolate too fast.
5. Chocolate accidents are rare.
6. Chocolate will not rust.
7. You do not need a key.
8. It is tougher for thieves to steal your chocolate.
9. Chocolate never hurts pedestrians.
10. You do not have to wax chocolate.

WHEN I GROW UP I WANT TO BE AN OOMPA-LOOMPA.

CRISPY CHOCOLATE CINNAMON STRIPS

Similar to churros. If you really like churros, buy a churros machine for your home for less than $50 online.

Difficulty: ♠♠♠
Preparation Time: 50 minutes
Yield: 24 strips

Cooking oil
½ lemon peel
½ cup butter or margarine
1 cup water
¼ teaspoon salt
1 cup flour, sifted
3 large eggs
⅓ cup sugar
1 teaspoon cinnamon

Dipping Chocolate:
½ cup semi-sweet chocolate chips
2 cups milk
1 teaspoon corn starch
4 teaspoons sugar

1. Add oil and lemon peel to deep fryer until 1½ inches deep. Heat to 375º.

2. In 3-quart saucepan, combine water, butter and salt. Bring to rolling boil. Reduce heat to low and stir in flour until mixture forms a ball of dough. Remove from heat.

3. Beat in eggs one at a time until dough is smooth and glossy.

4. Cool 5 minutes.

5. Prepare decorator bag fitted with large star nozzle. Spoon batter into decorator bag.

6. Squeeze four four-inch strips of dough into oil. Fry 3–4 minutes or until strips are golden brown. Remove from fryer and drain. Cool 5 minutes on paper towels.

7. Mix sugar and cinnamon.

8. Place crispy strips in 9x1½-inch pie pan and sprinkle with sugar and cinnamon mixture. (Another easy way to coat strips with mixture is to place mixture in a resealable one gallon bag, add strips and shake. This will ensure the strips are thoroughly covered.)

Dipping chocolate:

9. In double boiler, heat chocolate and 1 cup milk. Stir until chocolate melted. Reduce heat to low and add remaining milk and corn starch. Stir 5–7 minutes while chocolate thickens.

10. Remove from heat and pour chocolate into heat-proof dipping cups. Serve warm.

CHOCOLATE MARSHMALLOW PIE

Difficulty: ♠ ♠
Preparation Time: 20 minutes
Yield: 6 servings

½ pound mini-marshmallows
2 ounces German Sweet Chocolate
¾ cup low-fat milk
1 cup whipping cream
¾ teaspoon vanilla
1 graham cracker pie crust

1. In double boiler, combine and stir marshmallows, chocolate and milk until melted. Remove from heat and cool. When cool, add whipped cream and vanilla. Pour mixture into graham cracker crust.

2. Refrigerate at least 3 hours before serving.

You may choose to add a dollop of whipping cream and shaved chocolate to top of each pie piece when serving.

♠ How do you get two pounds of chocolate home from the store in a hot car?
Answer: Eat it in the parking lot.

♠ What did the gingerbread man do when his eyesight failed?
Answer: Bought contact chocolate chips.

1. Which came out first, the Mounds bar or Almond Joy bar?
   a) Mounds bar
   b) Almond Joy bar
   c) They came out together

2. Which of the following candy bars was introduced first in the market?
   a) Snickers
   b) Almond Joy
   c) Baby Ruth
   d) Butterfinger

3. The Hershey's Chocolate Bar was first made in:
   a) 1900
   b) 1905
   c) 1926
   d) 1929

4. Italians' favorite flavorings for chocolate are:
   a) Vanilla and cinnamon
   b) Dried fruits
   c) Almonds, chestnuts or hazelnuts
   d) Peanuts and almonds

5. The intensity of the cocoa bean affects the final flavor of the chocolate. Which variety of bean below has the strongest or harshest flavor?
   a) Java
   b) Arriba
   c) Caracas
   d) Para

♠ *Solutions on page 143*

WHITE CHOCOLATE MOUSSE

Difficulty: ♠ ♠
Preparation Time: 25 minutes
Yield: 8 servings

1 cup white chocolate chips
2 cups heavy whipping cream
1 ounce milk chocolate (optional)

1. In medium microwave-safe bowl, melt chocolate and ¼ cup cream on high 1 minute. Remove from microwave and stir. Microwave on high 1 minute more, remove and stir until chocolate completely melted. Set mixture aside and cool to room temperature.

2. In large, chilled bowl with electric mixer, beat remaining 1¾ cups cream until soft peaks form. Be careful not to over beat. Fold half of cream into chocolate mixture. Fold in remaining half of cream, being careful to ensure mixture remains fluffy.

3. Spoon dessert into 8 6-ounce ramekins.

4. Chill at least 1 hour.

5. Make chocolate curls by shaving milk chocolate with vegetable peeler.

6. Remove mousses from refrigerator. Sprinkle chocolate curls on top and serve.

Optional:

7. Top with fresh berries and garnish with mint sprig.

TANTALIZING Tidbits

♠ *Guinness World Records* reports that the largest cookie ever made was a chocolate chip cookie.

♠ Five chocolatiers worked fifteen hours a day for four weeks to create Hans Burie's Belgian Chocolate Car. The car was the same size as an actual Opel. It was made with milk, dark and white Belgium Callebaut chocolate and weighed 1800 pounds.

♠ The Northwest Fudge Factory.Com in Ontario, Canada created the largest piece of fudge. The giant slab of fudge weighed 2,002 pounds and measured 166 feet in length, 9 inches wide, and 3 inches high. The chocolate-and-vanilla-swirl fudge was displayed at the New Sudbury Mall in Ontario, Canada on May 4, 2002. According to *Guinness World Records*, the fudge took a total of eighty-six hours to prepare and mould.

♠ According to the *Guinness Book of World Records*, the largest box of chocolates ever made was a Frango mint chocolates box weighing 3,226 pounds created by Marshall Field's in Chicago, Illinois on November 14, 2002.

♠ On April 4, 1996, the Rotary Club of Piet Retief, KwaZulu-Natal, South Africa, made an Easter egg which was just over twenty-five feet high. Made of marshmallow and chocolate, it weighed 8,968 pounds and holds the Guinness World Record for the tallest Easter egg.

♠ According to *Guinness Book of World Records*, the Gremi Provincial de Patisseria, Confiteria i Bolleria School in Barcelona, Spain built the world's tallest chocolate model. The model was of a ship, and measured 27'10.5" tall, 42'8" long, and 8'2.5" wide.

I HAVE ACHIEVED CHOCOLATE NIRVANA!

PEPPERMINT PATTY BROWNIES

Difficulty: ♠ ♠
Preparation Time: 20 minutes
Yield: 32 brownies

5 large eggs
1½ cups butter or margarine, melted
3 cups sugar
1 tablespoon vanilla extract
2 cups flour
1 cup unsweetened cocoa
1 teaspoon baking powder
1 teaspoon salt
24 peppermint patties

1. Heat oven to 350°. Grease bottom and sides of 13x9x2-inch pan.

2. In large bowl with an electric mixer, beat eggs. Add butter, sugar and vanilla and continue to beat until well mixed.

3. In large bowl, combine flour, cocoa, baking powder and salt. Fold dry ingredients into the egg mixture and stir well.

4. Reserve 2 cups of batter.

5. Spread remaining batter in bottom of prepared pan.

6. Remove peppermint patties from wrappers and break in half. Space patties evenly in single layer on top of batter in pan.

7. Spread reserved 2 cups of batter over patties.

8. Bake 50 minutes or until brownies begin to pull away from sides of pan.

9. Cool completely or serve warm with ice cream.

♠ Decorate your home in yummy chocolate colors. Accent the brown tones with lime green, robin's egg blue, sunny yellow, blush pink and deep red.

CHOCOLATE
Challenge

_____ 1. The chocolate liquid called "chocolate liquor" is the basic material of all chocolate and cocoa products, and comes from ground nibs.

_____ 2. "Conching" is a process of rolling and kneading chocolate to give it a smoother and richer texture.

_____ 3. Chocolate cannot be frozen.

_____ 4. A white, filmy residue on chocolate is called a bloom.

_____ 5. Ballotin boxes are the deep boxes in which chocolate is packed.

_____ 6. Chocolate contains more than 300 known chemicals.

_____ 7. Dark chocolate is just as good for you as a glass of red wine.

_____ 8. Chocolate is good for dogs.

_____ 9. Dark chocolate is better for you than milk chocolate.

_____ 10. Domingo Ghirardelli discovered a way to transform ground cocoa beans into a nearly fat-free chocolate powder through collaboration with Milton Hershey.

_____ 11. Nougat is a popular chocolate filling that is a mixture of beaten egg whites, boiled sugar and nuts or candied fruit.

♠ *Solutions on pages 143-144*

CHOCOLATE RASPBERRY TERRINE

Difficulty: ♠ ♠ ♠ ♠
Preparation Time: 40 minutes
Yield: 10 servings

¾ cup butter, unsalted
2 cups semi-sweet chocolate chips
3 large egg whites, beaten
¾ cup heavy cream, beaten
1½ tablespoons sugar
1¼ cups raspberries, drained

Sauce:
1½ cups semi-sweet chocolate chips
6 tablespoons butter, unsalted
1½ cups heavy cream

1. Grease bottom and sides of 9x5x3-inch loaf pan.

2. In double boiler, melt butter and semi-sweet chocolate. Add beaten egg whites, whipped cream and sugar. Pour half of mixture into loaf pan.

3. Reserve 1 ounce of raspberries and spread remainder over chocolate layer. Top with remaining chocolate mixture.

4. Chill 1 hour or until firm.

Sauce:

5. In double boiler, melt chocolate, butter and cream. Remove from heat and cool until mixture thickens.

6. Remove terrine from loaf pan. Cover with sauce.

7. Chill until sauce firm. Slice and serve with reserved raspberries.

Bonus Quick Fix: Cover and store any unused portion of sauce in refrigerator. Serve warm or cold in dessert bowls. When serving cold, add whipping cream with raspberries or sliced strawberries.

TOFFEE

Difficulty: ♠ ♠
Preparation Time: 15 minutes
Yield: 8 servings

1 cup chopped walnuts
¾ cup brown sugar, packed
½ cup butter or margarine
½ cup semi-sweet chocolate chips

1. Grease bottom and sides of 8x8x2-inch pan.

2. Sprinkle nuts evenly across bottom of pan.

3. In 3-quart saucepan, combine sugar and margarine. Stirring constantly, cook over medium heat to soft crack stage. Remove from heat and carefully spread over nuts.

4. Sprinkle chocolate pieces on top and let soften. Once melted, spread chocolate evenly over toffee.

5. Refrigerate at least 1 hour. Break into pieces and serve.

Note: The soft crack stage is 290° on a candy thermometer. If you do not have a candy thermometer, this occurs after the butter has boiled out and the mixture begins to take on a smooth, dark appearance. Be careful not to leave it too long or the mixture will burn.

♠ A preacher visits an elderly woman from his congregation. As he sits on the couch, he notices a large bowl of peanuts on the coffee table.

"Mind if I have a few?" he asks.

"No, not at all," the woman replies.

They chat for an hour and as the preacher stands to leave, he realizes that instead of eating just a few peanuts, he emptied most of the bowl.

"I'm very sorry for eating all your peanuts. I really just meant to eat a few," states the preacher.

"Oh that's all right," replies the woman. "Ever since I lost my teeth all I can do is suck the chocolate off them."

DELICIOUS Declarations!

Other things are just food, but chocolate's chocolate.
♠ Patrick Skene Catling

"Chocolate is heavenly, mellow, sensual, deep, dark, sumptuous, gratifying, potent, dense, creamy, seductive, suggestive, rich, excessive, silky, smooth, luxurious, celestial. Chocolate is downfall, happiness, pleasure, love, ecstasy, fantasy…Chocolate makes us wicked, guilty, sinful, healthy, chic, happy."
♠ Elaine Sherman, *Madame Chocolate's Book of Divine Indulgences*

Caramels are only a fad. Chocolate is a permanent thing.
♠ Milton Snavely Hershey

For who could hate or bear a grudge against a luscious bit of fudge.
♠ Oompa-Loompas, *Willy Wonka and the Chocolate Factory*

All alone I send
To the one who is my Lord:
In this place where the gods command,
The flower-chocolate drink is foaming—the flower intoxication.
I yearn, oh yes!
For my heart has tasted it:
It intoxicated my heart—songs, dreams, yearnings.
My heart has tasted it.
♠ Tlaltecatzin, Aztec Poet

Think of chocolate like wine. As with wine, the world of chocolates is one of varietal distinctions, origins, unique blends, and manufacturing methods.
♠ Alice Medrich

The superiority of chocolate, both for health and nourishment, will soon give it the preference over tea and coffee in America which it has in Spain.
♠ Thomas Jefferson

CHOCOLATE TURTLE BARS

This recipe was adapted from a recipe by neighbor Marsh Peters.

Difficulty: ♠ ♠ ♠
Preparation Time: 35 minutes
Yield: 32 pieces

1⅓ cups butter, melted
2 cups flour
2 cups oatmeal
1½ cups brown sugar
1 teaspoon baking soda
¾ teaspoon salt
1 pound of caramels
7 tablespoons heavy cream
1½ cups chocolate chips
½ cup pecans or other nut, chopped (optional)

1. Heat oven to 350º. Grease bottom and sides of 13x9x2-inch pan.

2. In large bowl, mix together butter, flour, oatmeal, sugar, baking soda and salt. Press half of mixture into pan.

3. Bake 10 minutes.

4. In 4-quart saucepan over medium heat, melt together caramels and cream.

5. Remove pan from oven and sprinkle chocolate chips and pecans on top of baked mixture.

6. Evenly pour melted caramels and milk on top.

7. Spread reserved mixture evenly on top of caramels and bake 15 minutes.

8. Cool completely before serving. You may wish to chill in refrigerator.

♠ There is never a wrong time for chocolate.

QUICK FIX

🔹 Chow Mein Clusters*

🔹 Cookies & Cream Roll

🔹 Fruit Sorbet

🔹 Fudge in a Hurry

🔹 Mocha Coffee

🔹 Mocha Shake

🔹 No-bake Oatmeal Cookies

🔹 Peanut Butter Balls

🔹 Peanut Butter & Butterscotch Bars

🔹 Potato Chips

🔹 Pudding

🔹 Raspberry Dream

🔹 Raspberry Trifle

🔹 Rocky Road

🔹 Soup

🔹 Spiced Drink

🔹 Tacos

🔹 Tortilla

🔹 Watermelon

🔹 Yogurt

CHOCOLATE CHOW MEIN CLUSTERS

Difficulty: ♠
Preparation Time: 9 minutes
Yield: 18 clusters

¾ cup semi-sweet chocolate chips
1 cup butterscotch chips
2 cups chow mein noodles
1 cup salted peanuts (optional)

1. Line 2 cookie sheets with wax paper.

2. In medium microwave-safe bowl, melt chocolate and butterscotch chips on high 90 seconds. Stir until smooth. Mix in chow mein noodles and peanuts.

3. Drop heaping tablespoons onto cookie sheets.

4. Chill in refrigerator 7 minutes or until set.

COOKIE & CREAM ROLL

Difficulty: ♠
Preparation Time: 5 minutes
Yield: 4 servings

8 ounces whipped cream
16 thin chocolate wafers or cookies

1. Line 9x5x3-inch loaf pan with aluminum foil.

2. Spread layer of whipped cream across foil.

3. At one end of pan, vertically place 1 cookie on top of whipped cream; cookie should be standing on its edge. Spread whipped cream on back of cookie (facing toward the inside of pan).

4. Place next cookie vertically in pan, touching whipped cream from first cookie. Spread whipped cream on back of new cookie.

5. Repeat until all cookies have been used.

6. Cover top and sides with whipped cream and freeze dessert roll.

7. To serve, remove from freezer and slice vertically. Set portion upright on plate and drizzle chocolate syrup over top.

FRUIT SORBET CHOCOLATE CUPS

Difficulty: ♠
Preparation Time: 5 minutes
Yield: 8 servings

2½ cups frozen raspberries or strawberries
½ cup sugar
¾ cup plain yogurt
8 dark chocolate dessert cups

1. Place berries and sugar in blender. Blend on high speed 20 seconds or until berries are chopped into smaller pieces. Add yogurt. Pulse until mixed.

2. Spoon sorbet into chocolate cups.

3. Freeze at least 2 hours before serving.

FUDGE IN A HURRY

Difficulty: ♠
Preparation Time: 10 minutes
Yield: 2 pounds

1½ cups semi-sweet chocolate chips, melted
14 ounces condensed milk
1 cup pecans or walnuts, chopped
1½ teaspoons vanilla

1. Grease and flour cookie sheet.

2. In large bowl, stir together melted chocolate, condensed milk, walnuts and vanilla.

3. Spread onto cookie sheet.

4. Cool before serving.

MOCHA COFFEE

Difficulty: ♠
Preparation Time: 8 minutes
Yield: 4 servings

4 teaspoons instant coffee
2 tablespoons cocoa powder
2 tablespoons nonfat dry milk
1 teaspoon ground cinnamon
½ teaspoon dried orange peel
4 cups boiling water
1 teaspoon chocolate, finely grated (optional)

1. In small bowl, mix coffee, cocoa powder, nonfat dry milk, ground cinnamon and orange peel.

2. In large microwave-safe bowl, heat water on high until boiling.

3. Add coffee mixture to boiling water and stir. Pour into 4 coffee mugs.

4. Garnish with finely grated chocolate. Serve immediately.

MOCHA SHAKE

Difficulty: ♠
Preparation Time: 5 minutes
Yield: 4 servings

2 cups milk
1 pint chocolate ice cream
⅛ teaspoon almond extract
1½ tablespoons instant coffee
¼ cup chocolate syrup
Whipped topping (optional)

1. Combine and blend first five ingredients in a blender.

2. Pour into glasses and add whipped topping, if desired.

For a Mocha Float: Combine first 4 ingredients above. Add an additional 2 cups of milk and replace ¼ cup chocolate syrup with ¼ cup sugar. Blend and pour into glasses. Add one scoop of vanilla ice cream to the top of each glass. Serves 6.

PEANUT BUTTER BALLS

Difficulty: ♠
Preparation Time: 10 minutes
Yield: 18 balls

1 cup creamy peanut butter
1½ cups instant powdered milk
4 tablespoons honey
¼ cup milk chocolate chips
¼ cup white chocolate chips
½ cup semi-sweet chocolate chips (optional)

1. In medium bowl, mix peanut butter, milk and honey. Stir until dough is smooth.

2. Use heaping teaspoon to form batter into 1-inch round balls. Place on ungreased cookie sheet or plate.

3. Eat!

But wait...you can enhance your eating experience: In small microwave-safe bowl, melt semi-sweet chocolate chips in microwave. Quickly dip peanut butter balls in chocolate and place on wax paper. Refrigerate 10 minutes to let chocolate harden.

♠ Top 10 Reasons Why Chocolate is Better Than a Blind Date:

1. Chocolate is always compatible.
2. You do not have to dress up for chocolate.
3. Chocolate will not be late.
4. Chocolate can be short or tall, and it is still perfect.
5. Chocolate will not tell corny jokes.
6. Chocolate will not take you to a dumb movie.
7. Chocolate will not bore you.
8. Chocolate will not run out of gas or get a flat tire.
9. Chocolate will not ask you for money.
10. Chocolate does not expect a good night kiss.

PEANUT BUTTER & BUTTERSCOTCH BARS

Difficulty: ♠
Preparation Time: 12 minutes
Yield: 18 bars

½ cup sugar
½ cup light corn syrup
¾ cup peanut butter
3 cups crisp rice cereal
1 cup milk chocolate chips
½ cup butterscotch chips

1. Grease bottom and sides of 13x9x2-inch pan.

2. In large microwave-safe bowl, heat sugar and corn syrup on high 2 minutes. Immediately add peanut butter and cereal. Mix well.

3. In small microwave-safe bowl, heat chocolate and butterscotch chips on high 2 minutes. Stir. If not completely melted, microwave an additional 30 seconds.

4. Stir chocolate mixture into peanut butter and cereal mixture.

5. Spread mixture in prepared pan and flatten with back side of a spoon.

6. Place in refrigerator 15 minutes and let harden.

Another tasty recipe alternative: Reserve chocolate mixture for topping. Follow initial steps of recipe, and complete peanut butter and cereal mixture. Spoon into prepared pan. With a knife, spread chocolate mixture across top.

Note: Add chocolate mixture to peanut butter and cereal mixture right away or the sugar and corn syrup will harden, making it difficult to mix.

CHOCOLATE POTATO CHIPS

Difficulty: ♠
Preparation time: 10 minutes
Yield: 4 servings

1 bag ridged potato chips
¾ cup semi-sweet chocolate chips, melted

1. Carefully dip chips halfway into melted chocolate. Place on wax paper and let set until chocolate hardens.

You can also dip cookies, candy bars, banana chips and so much more. Enjoy!

HOMEMADE CHOCOLATE PUDDING

Difficulty: ♠
Preparation Time: 15 minutes
Yield: 8 servings

2 cups sugar
4 tablespoons cornstarch
4 cups low-fat milk
¾ cup semi-sweet chocolate chips
2 teaspoons vanilla extract

1. In 3-quart saucepan over medium heat, combine sugar and cornstarch.

2. In medium microwave-safe bowl, heat milk on high 30 seconds. Stir into sugar mixture.

3. Stir mixture over medium heat until sugar dissolves and mixture begins to boil.

4. Turn heat to medium-low and add chocolate. Stir until chocolate is melted and mixture thickens. Remove from heat and cool 5 minutes.

5. Stir in vanilla.

6. Pour into 8 6-ounce ramekins and serve immediately.

CHOCOLATE RASPBERRY TRIFLE

Difficulty: ♠ ♠
Preparation Time: 15 minutes
Yield: 10 servings

1½ cups low-fat milk
3–4 ounces instant chocolate pudding
3¼ cups whipped topping
¼ cup apricot fruit spread
1 twelve-ounce pound cake
2 cups raspberries

1. Cut cake into ten even slices.

2. With a knife, apply fruit spread to top of 5 of the cake slices.

3. Cover fruited cake slices with remaining slices so they make a sandwich. Cut cakes into half-inch squares.

4. In large bowl with electric mixer, beat milk and pudding mix 3 minutes or until well blended. Stir in 1 cup whipped topping.

5. Layer bottom of a large serving dish with half of the cake squares. Cover squares with half of the berries. Pour half of the pudding mix over berries.

6. Add remaining cake squares on top. Cover with remaining berries and whipped topping.

7. Serve immediately.

♠ What is an elk-like animal that runs through a chocolate factory?
Answer: Chocolate Mousse.

ROCKY ROAD (HEAVENLY HASH)

Difficulty: ♠
Preparation Time: 10 minutes
Yield: 24 pieces

1½ cups milk chocolate chips, melted
¾ cup pecans or other nut, chopped
1¾ cups miniature marshmallows.

1. In large bowl, combine all ingredients. Mix well.

2. Drop by heaping teaspoonfuls on tray lined with wax paper.

3. Cool before serving.

CHOCOLATE SOUP

Difficulty: ♠
Preparation Time: 7 minutes
Yield: 6 servings

8 ounces white or semi-sweet chocolate, chopped
⅛ teaspoon salt
1 cup low-fat milk
1 cup heavy cream

1. In medium microwave-safe bowl, heat chocolate and salt on high 1 minute. Stir.

2. In small microwave-safe bowl, heat milk and cream on high 1½ minutes.

3. Pour one-third cream mixture over chocolate. Stir or whisk until well blended.

4. Stir in reserved cream mixture until well blended.

5. Heat in microwave on medium until very hot.

6. Divide among bowls. Serve immediately.

SPICED CHOCOLATE DRINK

Difficulty: ♠
Preparation Time: 5 minutes
Yield: 2 servings

1½ cups low-fat milk
1 cup vanilla ice cream
6 tablespoons chocolate syrup
¼ teaspoon ground cinnamon
¼ teaspoon ground cloves
¼ teaspoon ground nutmeg
Grated chocolate (optional)

1. In blender, combine all ingredients on high 30 seconds or until mixture is smooth.

2. Chill 2 glasses and pour half of drink into each glass.

3. Garnish with grated chocolate. Serve immediately.

CHOCOLATE TACOS

Difficulty: ♠
Preparation Time: 3 minutes
Yield: 2 servings

2 frozen waffles
2 cups chocolate ice cream
2 tablespoons chocolate syrup
Fresh raspberries or strawberries (optional)
Whipped cream (optional)
Peanuts or other nut, chopped (optional)
2 maraschino cherries (optional)

1. Toast frozen waffles.

2. When done, remove from toaster and place heaping scoop of chocolate ice cream on top of each waffle.

3. Pick up waffle from sides and eat like a taco.

CHOCOLATE TORTILLA

Difficulty: ♠
Preparation Time: 3 minutes
Yield: 8 servings

8 flour tortillas
16 ounces chocolate frosting

1. Spread chocolate frosting on one side of tortilla.

2. Fold in half like a taco with chocolate inside.

3. Eat and enjoy—sandwiches don't get much better than this!

NO-BAKE CHOCOLATE OATMEAL COOKIES

Difficulty: ♠
Preparation Time: 12 minutes
Yield: 36 cookies

2 cups sugar
½ cup butter or margarine
½ cup low-fat milk
1 teaspoon vanilla
3 tablespoons cocoa powder
½ cup chunky peanut butter
3½ cups oatmeal

1. In 3-quart saucepan, combine sugar, butter and milk. Boil over medium heat 2–3 minutes.

2. Remove from heat and add remaining ingredients. Mix well.

3. Drop by heaping teaspoonful onto wax paper and cool.

4. Refrigerate 1 hour and serve.

CHOCOLATE CRUNCH YOGURT

Difficulty: ♠
Preparation Time: 3 minutes
Yield: 2 servings

2 cups yogurt
¼ cup semi-sweet chocolate chips

1. Stir chocolate chips into yogurt.

2. Serve in two bowls.

For a truly invigorating experience: Subsitute raw chocolate (cacao nibs) for the chocolate chips. You can normally purchase cacao nibs at organic food stores. Cacao nibs are the crushed beans from which chocolate is made. Raw chocolate can be enjoyed by itself, substituted for chocolate chips, or shaken on top of oatmeal, high-grain cereals and other foods that need a little livening up.

RASPBERRY DREAM

Difficulty: ♠
Preparation Time: 10 minutes
Yield: 4 servings

4 ounces raspberries
¼ cup semi-sweet chocolate chips
8 tablespoons chocolate syrup

1. Wash raspberries. Place one or two chocolate chips in cavity at top of each raspberry.

2. Spoon raspberries onto plates, placing approximately one ounce of raspberries onto each plate.

3. Drizzle 2 tablespoons chocolate syrup on each serving. Delicious!

A tasty alternative that requires a bit of patience: After placing chocolate chips in raspberry cavitiy, place raspberries in refrigerator for 1 hour. Remove and serve immediately with or without chocolate.

CHOCOLATE WATERMELON

Difficulty: ♠
Preparation Time: 15 minutes
Yield: 8 servings

1 quart lime sherbet, softened
1 quart raspberry sherbet, softened
⅔ cup semi-sweet chocolate chips

1. Line 2-quart glass bowl with plastic wrap.

2. Forming a shell, press lime sherbet against bottom and sides of bowl. Place bowl in freezer 10 minutes or until sherbet firms.

3. In blender or mixing bowl, combine raspberry sherbet and chocolate chips. Scoop mixture into center of lime sherbet mold

4. Cover and freeze at least 6 hours.

5. To serve, invert glass bowl on serving plate. Remove plastic wrap and slice like a watermelon.

GOOD NEWS! YOU'RE ONLY ALLERGIC TO LIMA BEANS AND CHOCOLATE.

PHYSICAL ACTIVITY

The US Department of Agriculture (USDA) recommends physical activity as part of the new Food Guide Pyramid. Here are some suggestions:

♠ Whisk ingredients briskly. Rotate direction every 20 times around the bowl. Switch arms and repeat.

♠ Expedite the cooling process of your chocolate baked goods by flailing your arms in a windmill fashion. Switch direction every 20 flails.

♠ Take brisk walks to and from the market to purchase more chocolate.

♠ Celebrate each finished chocolate masterpiece you prepare by developing your own special kitchen dance. You may also want to perform this dance while serving your dish to guests.

♠ While grating and zesting, exhale on the downstroke and inhale on the way up.

♠ Juice fruits without the assistance of any gadgets. Squeeze, release, squeeze, release…

♠ Even after your chocolate is in the oven, repeat your "oven-door hip closing" move 20 times on the right. Rotate and repeat on the left.

♠ Strategically place ingredients on opposite countertops. Use lunges to retrieve them.

♠ Do the cast-iron skillet lift: Place skillet on stovetop. Grasp handle with right hand and raise it to shoulder height. Repeat 10 times. Switch to left hand and repeat.

♠ Lastly, exercise those mandibles by chewing all of your chocolate with vigor. Mmm…delicious!

♠ SOLUTIONS ♠

GRAINS CHALLENGES

♠ Page 4

1. (e) All of the above
2. (b) One year
3. (d) Unsweetened chocolate
4. (b) Fatbloom

♠ Page 15

1. (True) This is true according to *The Emperors of Chocolate*.
2. (False) The first Tootsie Roll was produced in 1896. The Tootsie Pop was invented in 1931.
3. (False) Curtis Candy Company named Baby Ruth in honor of president Grover Cleveland's baby daughter.
4. (False) Forrest invented M&M's during the Spanish Civil War after he watched soldiers eat chocolate with a hard sugary coating. M&M's were first sold in 1941.
5. (False) Hershey's makes approximately 20–25 million Kisses daily.
6. (False) According to the National Candy Buyers Brands Survey, Snickers is the most popular candy bar in the United States.
7. (True) The chocolate chip cookie was invented in 1930 at the Toll House Restaurant in Whitman, Massachusetts.
8. (False) Approximately 91% prefer milk chocolate, but dark chocolate's popularity is growing rapidly.
9. (True)
10. (True)

VEGETABLES CHALLENGES

♠ Page 27
   1. (d) 150 feet
   2. (b) 875,000
   3. (d) Dark chocolate

♠ Page 30
   1. (True) The Hershey's Kiss-shaped lights light the sidewalks of "Chocolate Avenue."
   2. (True)
   3. (True) A chocoholic is defined as "a person who craves or compulsively consumes chocolate."
   4. (True) This changed when a technique for making solid chocolate was devised.
   5. (True)
   6. (True)
   7. (True)
   8. (False) Boxes featuring inlaid semi-precious stones and stunning paintings became vogue as early as 1780.

♠ Page 35
   1. (a) Virtually fat-free chocolate powder
   2. (b) Ethel M. Chocolates
   3. (d) All of the above
   4. (c) Great Britain
   5. (e) All of the above

FRUITS CHALLENGES

♠ Page 50
   1. (c) Forastero beans; they are more plentiful, easier to cultivate, and have a pungent aroma.
   2. (d) Hawaii
   3. (a) Ivory Coast, Africa
   4. (d) Africa; they produce nearly twice the tonnage of South America.
   5. (d) Bittersweet chocolate; it contains at least 35% chocolate liquor, usually around 50%.

1. (b) Reese's Peanut Butter Cup
2. (c) Snickers
3. (d) Twix
4. (d) Almond Joy
5. (c) Butterfinger

MILK CHALLENGES

♠ Page 66
1. (b) White wine; Chocolate tends to mask the aroma and flavor of wine.
2. (b) Dark chocolate
3. (a) Tempering by hand
4. (b) Drink of the gods

♠ Page 72
1. (d) All of the above
2. (d) 13,183 pounds
3. (a) Halloween
4. (b) 1765; the pair built the factory in Massachusetts.
5. (b) London; prior to that time only nobility could afford to drink chocolate.

MEATS, BEANS & NUTS CHALLENGES

♠ Page 85
1. (d) *Every 1's A Winner*; the song hit the charts in 1979.
2. (d) *Willy Wonka and the Chocolate Factory*; was released first in 1971, followed by *Bread and Chocolate* in 1973, *Like Water for Chocolate* in 1992, and *Chocolat* in 2000.
3. (e) All of the above
4. (d) White Chocolate

♠ Page 93
1. (False) "El Chocolate" was a famous flamenco singer.
2. (True)
3. (True) According to historical records, he ate chocolate whenever he needed quick energy.
4. (True) According to various accounts, Emperor Montezuma drank 50 or more portions of "chocolatl" daily.
5. (True) He founded the Hershey Chocolate Company in 1894.
6. (True) Godiva was founded in Brussels, Belgium by master chocolatier Joseph Draps. He named the company in honor of the legend of Lady Godiva.

FATS & SWEETS CHALLENGES

♠ Page 114
1. (a) Mounds bar; it was created in 1921. It took twenty-six more years for the Almond Joy bar to come out in 1947.
2. (c) Baby Ruth; this candy bar was first introduced in 1920, followed by Butterfinger in 1923, Snickers in 1930, and Almond Joy in 1947.
3. (a) 1900
4. (c) Italians prefer a nutty flavor.
5. (d) Java, Arriba and Caracas are mild varieties, while Para has a stronger taste.

♠ Page 119
1. (True) Nibs are the "meat" of the cocoa bean
2. (True) The longer chocolate is conched, the more luxurious it will feel on your tongue.
3. (False) Chocolate can be frozen by wrapping it in freezer paper and placing it in two plastic bags. To defrost, remove from the freezer and slowly bring to room temperature; this will eliminate condensation.
4. (True) A bloom usually occurs when chocolate is stored in a warm area. Chocolate is best stored at 68–72° Fahrenheit.
5. (True)
6. (True) Scientists continue to study these chemicals to determine which combinations may explain some of the pleasurable effects of consuming chocolate.

7. (True) Research shows that dark chocolate and red wine contain flavonoid phenolics which are known to lower the risk of heart disease. Cocoa is approximately 20% protein, 40% carbohydrate, and 40% fat.
8. (False) Theobromine in chocolate stimulates the cardiac and nervous systems and can be lethal to dogs, especially smaller pups.
9. (True) Researchers in Scotland and Italy say that dark chocolate has much better antioxidant properties.
10. (False) He discovered it by accident. One of his factory workers accidentally left a cloth bag with ground cocoa beans hanging from a hook. The cocoa butter separated and dripped through the bottom of the bag, leaving a nearly fat-free chocolate powder.
11. (True) Nougat is a popular chocolate filling made as described.